Finding Your Perfect Mate

H. Norman Wright

HARVEST HOUSE PUBLISHERS
Eugene, Oregon 97402

FINDING YOUR PERFECT MATE

Copyright © 1995 by Harvest House Publishers
Eugene, Oregon 97402

Library of Congress Cataloging-in-Publication Data

Wright, H. Norman
    Finding your perfect mate / H. Norman Wright.
      p. cm.
    ISBN 1-56507-237-5
    1. Mate selection—Religious aspects—Christianity. 2. Man-woman relationships—Religious aspects—Christianity. 3. Interpersonal relations— Religious aspects—Christianity. I. Title.
HQ801.W84 1995
646.7'.7—dc20   94-47486
                                                   CIP

97   98   99   00   01 — 10 9 8 7 6 5

Contents

Marriage—
Is It the Answer for You?

*I*t sounds like such a long time ago—
1959! Two months out of college and a month away from
graduate school, I took the plunge—marriage. Twenty-
two years of being single came to an end. I really looked
forward to marriage. Did I actually know what to expect?
No. Did I know how to function as a husband? Not
really. So, I guess you could say I wasn't fully prepared
for what I encountered. That's true. But I began to learn,
and it's continued over 35 years.

Marriage—you're wanting to be married or you
wouldn't be reading at this point. In fact, you're looking
for that perfect specimen who will be everything you
want and will meet all of your needs and unspoken
requests. *But you're not going to find such a person!* Every
prospect you find will be flawed and incompatible with
you. But that's all right. We all began marriage with the
same conditions. Keep searching, but realize that even
with the best match you find, you won't really be

compatible in the beginning. However, you can *become* compatible. Plan on that as a major marriage goal for the first five to ten years. That's what it takes if you work at it. If you don't, you may never learn to mesh together. That's alarming, isn't it? I want you to be alarmed! I want you to be aware of what it takes to be married and to make it a fulfilling experience for you. Let's think about you and marriage for a while.

If you're considering marriage, you must have some hopes and dreams about it. Exactly what is it that you're hoping marriage is going to do for you? When I worked with a number of college departments and singles' groups in churches, I asked a question in this form: "What will you get out of marriage that you wouldn't get if you were to remain single?" It's a question to think about, pray about, and discuss with a trusted friend or several married couples for realistic clarification. Please notice the word *realistic*!

What Happens When You Marry

When you marry, you and your spouse will experience a momentous head-on collision if you expect to bring your life as you now know it into marriage and continue its existence. Each of you will need to do some housecleaning and abandon your world as you know it now, so you can form a new life and a new culture. Most of us aren't expecting that drastic a transition. But you're not marrying a clone who thinks, acts, and does things just like you. So who gives in, changes, and adapts? Which way is best? You'll have to discover that together. It's so much easier to confront as many of these issues as possible before you marry, rather than to be devastated and disillusioned by them after the wedding. As one man said, "Marriage is not a 50-50 proposition. It's more like a 90-10 relationship. Sometimes you give 90, and sometimes you get 90. But don't try and keep score."

Getting married will change your dating relationship. All of the conscious and unconscious expectations you brought with you will now be tested, and some will be found wanting. The act of marriage acts as a trigger to unleash all the underlying hopes, fears, needs, and desires that have been lying dormant for years awaiting the time they could be exposed.

If you question whether or not getting married brings about significant changes, think about this. In a major national survey of what happened during the first year of marriage, 50 to 60 percent of the newlyweds (and half of them had lived together prior to marriage) reported the following:

—The number of arguments they had changed after they were married.

—Their tendency to be critical of one another changed (most were more critical).

—Their feelings of self-confidence changed.

—Their relationship with their own family changed.

—Their attitude toward their work changed.

—Their interest in having an attractive home changed.[1]

In addition, between 40 and 50 percent said they had occasional doubts whether their marriage would last, had significant marital problems, and reported discovering that being married was harder than they ever thought it would be.[2]

This same survey found a disturbing and sobering fact that could be very beneficial for those planning to marry. There were as many regrets about the first year of marriage as people who have been married. Almost everyone wished they had done something differently.

The most frequently mentioned factor concerned developing goals and specifying their needs before marriage. They wished they had assumed more responsibility for the success of the relationship.[3]

Of those in this survey who divorced, all of them said the problems began at the beginning of their marriage, but many denied or ignored the problems until it was too late.[4]

Sounds overwhelming and almost impossible, doesn't it? Well, on your own it is. I don't know how couples ever work it out without learning to submit to God. Claire Cloninger, in her book *When the Glass Slipper Doesn't Fit and the Silver Spoon Is in Someone Else's Mouth*, described the miracle of marriage extremely well:

> I figure that the degree of difficulty in combining two lives ranks somewhere between rerouting a hurricane and finding a parking place in downtown Manhattan. I am of the opinion that only God Himself can make a marriage happen really well. And when He does it His way, it's one of His very best miracles. I mean, the Red Sea was good, but for my money this is better. What God can create out of...two surrendered lives is "infinitely more than we ever dare to ask or imagine."[5]

Through Him we can discover how to experience His grace in our marriage. Along with the abandonment of your single lifestyle is the need to abandon yourself to His will and His strength as you proceed through your marriage. There may be days in which no matter how well you prepared for your marriage you may stop and say, "This isn't exactly what I expected. Was this the best decision for me? I thought so at that time." When this happens, that's where the depth of realistic love (which is discussed in a later chapter) and commitment will have to sustain your marriage.

In a book of essays on marriage, Mike Mason wrote, "Marriage involves a continuous daily renewal of a decision which, since it is of such a staggering order as to be humanly impossible to make, can only be made through the grace of God."[6]

The Results of Living Together Before Marriage

What about living together? Many couples feel that's the solution and will prevent divorce. One of the most damaging myths to aid in the destruction of long-term marriage is that "living together before marriage will give a couple a better foundation for marriage." In every research study this pattern has been found to be deadly to the marriage relationship. To be blunt, when a couple lives together before marriage they can expect failure. The divorce rate is significantly higher for these couples. To give you a perspective on what happens to such couples, of 100 couples who began living together, 40 of them will break up before marriage. Of the 60 who marry, at least 35 will divorce, which leaves 25 out of the original 100 who make it.[7]

Many who read this amazing result will say, "But we're the exception. We're different. We'll make it." But those who protest so loudly usually become a statistic.

When couples live together there is a denial of reality that divorce could happen to them. Living with another person is not the same as auditioning for a part in a play and hoping to get it. You don't play house and audition for the part of a husband or wife. When you live together or are just sexually active, your objectivity in decision-making becomes clouded. I've seen this with many couples. When a couple becomes sexually active or lives together prior to marriage, it makes it difficult to make objective decisions or rationally view the problem areas. It's much easier to learn and discern when you're dating than when you're sexual or living together.

It is impossible to duplicate the process of marriage by living together. There is always that underlying attitude, "This is a test. This is a trial run. Let's find the problems now so I can bail out of this relationship." This is a far cry from "Let's find the problems so we can work on them and learn to be compatible." When you live together there is a limit of what you invest, not only emotionally but financially as well. You don't usually have children, and there is a sense of awkwardness and uncomfortableness around other people with different values. There is still a limited and selective acceptance of this involvement depending upon the group you're with. It's like trying to be somewhat married but without the rules.

When you live together you reflect an ambivalence. You don't want the single lifestyle nor do you want marriage. It's not the best of both worlds. It is actually worse. You're single, but you don't have the freedom to cultivate new relationships. You're not single anymore. But you're not fully married, so you cannot develop intimacy to its fullest degree either. There's a cloud of uncertainty that hangs over the relationship.[8]

Living together doesn't give you the opportunity to build intimacy; rather, it brings up issues of who shops, who cooks, who cleans, etc. You have one foot in the relationship and one foot out.

Premarital Sexual Involvement— Reasons to Wait

These next statements are what I call "toe-steppers," but they need to be said. When couples live together or have a sexual relationship, not only does it cloud the decision-making process, it also reflects the attitude of less mature, "instant gratification" people. The greater the level of maturity, the more you are able to delay gratification and establish healthy boundaries. You feel good about yourself and your identity.

Living together is usually more of a convenience for the man than the woman. A women tends to live together with a man to be wanted and taken care of. A lot of energy is exerted trying to determine "Is this going to work?" after you move in, instead of saying, "Yes, we will make this work!"

I've already mentioned the problem of instant gratification in premature sexual involvement. But there are three other major reasons to wait until marriage before engaging in sexual intercourse. One is the clear teaching of Scripture. If you are involved with a person who says that the Bible isn't for today or that it doesn't teach sexual purity prior to marriage, you are involved with someone who is either biblically illiterate, or puts his/her own desires ahead of God's plan—or both!

A second reason has already been mentioned: It clouds the rationality needed to make wise decisions.

But the third reason is that sexually active individuals are more likely to divorce. The sociological evidence indicates that non-virgins increase their odds for divorce by about 60 percent.[9]

Jim Talley in *Too Close, Too Soon* gives an interesting insight concerning the sexual relationship. In his book, written with Bobbie Reed, he notes that "men and women have a tendency to approach intimacy differently. For men, physical intimacy often precedes emotional involvement; however, women usually relate emotionally before they are physically close to a dating partner." This creates inevitable misunderstandings.

> If a woman believes that physical contact follows emotional intimacy, then she may assume her partner to be as emotionally committed to the relationship as she. . . . She may start expecting a marriage proposal once her partner initiates physical intimacy. Perfectly logical to her; possibly terrifying to him. The relationship may end at this

point. The man, completely surprised by the depth of his partner's emotional attachment to him...may withdraw, explaining that he isn't ready for a serious relationship.

True intimacy takes time to develop as trust is built into each facet of a relationship by a series of shared experiences.... Recognizing and accepting the fact that physical and emotional intimacies tend to have different priorities for men and women is the first step in resolving those differences. The second step is to exercise mutual patience.[10]

Of course, patience is *not* the characteristic of most modern romances—sexual intimacy is the norm, and it is like putting rocket boosters on a Ford and shooting it down a highway at high speed. Dr. Talley uses another image to describe the danger:

Premarital sex creates instability in the relationship. It is like trying to build the second floor of a building on a few sticks in the ground. There is guilt, an unrealistic expectation of marriage, when neither made that commitment, and an intensity in the relationship without a foundation of friendship to hold it up.[11]

You may say, "It's not only too difficult to abstain, it's an impossibility. It's unrealistic. It's unnatural." Really? Consider this:

The attitude of much of society seems to be that our sexual appetite *must be satisfied.* We're told that normal, healthy life requires it. We have to eat, drink, and have intercourse to live. But that's simple falsehood. It is possible to live a fully normal, healthy, and happy life without sexual intercourse. You'll die if you don't eat and drink, but you won't die if you abstain from sex. It's the failure (perhaps I should say refusal) to recognize this fact that makes it impossible for many people to honestly consider self-control in regard to their sexual life. Self-control is not only possible, it's also required of the Christian single. It's God's rule of life for us, and we must seek it if we mean to walk with Him.

Let me suggest some things that will help in the struggle for self-control.

First, self-control is simply impossible for the person who refuses to make a commitment to it. Self-control begins with a hard and clear decision to be a certain kind of person. The single person who toys around with his commitment is simply guaranteeing his failure, but the person who honestly determines that he will refrain from sexual intercourse is going to have success.

I want to emphasize the *certainty of success* for those who make a personal commitment to refrain from intercourse. A real commitment made by a person who knows himself well will bring success. I'm talking of a life-and-death determination.[12]

Factors That Make a Marriage Work

What are some factors that will bring about a marriage that survives?

Those couples who have fulfilling marriages put their partner as the number-one person in their life, and their family of origin (parents and siblings) is now secondary. They have either separated from them emotionally in a healthy way or have made peace with whatever the issues have been. They now function as adults without dependence upon their original family.

Commitment

The glue that will keep marriage together is not love. There is a word that is becoming foreign in meaning and application to our culture in general—it's the word *commitment*. Oh, I hear many people who say they can commit to someone or something, and their commitment is in place when everything is going well. It's when things get tough that the true level of commitment is evident.

Marriage is an unconditional commitment and not a contract. Some psychologists, marriage counselors, and ministers have suggested that marriage *is* a contract, and many people are quick to agree. But is this true? Is marriage really a contract?

In every contract there are certain conditional clauses. A contract between two parties, whether they be companies or individuals, involves the responsibility of both parties to carry out their part of the bargain. These are conditional clauses or "if" clauses. If you do *this*, the other person must do *this*, and if the other person does *this*, you must do *this*. But in the marriage relationship there are no conditional clauses. Nowhere in the marriage ceremony does the pastor say, "If the husband loves his wife, then the wife continues in the contract." Or, "If the wife is submissive to her husband, then the husband carries out the contract." Marriage is an unconditional commitment into which two people enter.

In most contracts there are escape clauses. An escape clause says that if the party of the first part does not carry out his responsibilities, then the party of the second part is absolved. If one person does not live up to his part of the bargain, the second person can get out of the contract. This is an escape clause. In marriage there is no escape clause.

Commitment means many things to different people. For some, the strength of their commitment varies with how they feel emotionally or physically. The word *commit* is a verb and means "to do or to perform." It is a binding pledge or promise. It is a private pledge you also make public. It is a pledge carried out to completion, running over any roadblocks. It is a total giving of oneself to another person. Yes, it is risky, but it makes life fulfilling.

Perhaps a better way to describe this is to compare it to bungee jumping. If you've ever taken the plunge, you know that when you take that step off the platform you are committed to following through. There is no more time to think it over or change your mind. There is no turning back.

A friend of mine shared with me what has made his marriage last. He said, "Norm, we each had a commitment to each other and to the marriage. When our commitment to each other was low, it was the commitment to the marriage that kept us together."

Commitment to another person until he or she dies seems idealistic to some. When it suits us and we're not inconvenienced by the commitment, we keep it. But when certain problems occur, it's not valid. Commitment is more than continuing to stick it out and suffer with a poor choice of a spouse. It's not just maintaining; it's investing. It's not just enduring; it's working to make the relationship grow. It's not just accepting and tolerating negative and destructive patterns on the part of your spouse; it's working toward change. It's sticking to someone regardless of circumstances. Listen to one wife's story.

In 1988, I was diagnosed with Epstein Barr Virus (Chronic Fatigue Syndrome). It really changed my life, which had been filled with excitement and vibrancy. My husband Kelly has stood with me and become my protector through these past years of adjustment. He has taken care of our family, when my strength would not allow me. He has held my hand through depression, including 10 days in the hospital. He has insisted I get needed rest, even if it puts more of a burden on him. He has paid the price of any hopeful cure we have found, no matter the cost. He has been more than a husband, he has been my best friend. A friend that has stayed closer than any family member. He was my "knight in shining armor when I met him" and he has proven to be so throughout our 14 ½ years of marriage. I sometimes tell him that he has been "my salvation," because I don't know that I would still be going on, if it weren't for his strength. I don't know that I would still walk with the Lord, if it were not for his encouragement. Knowing him has been the greatest experience in my life.

If you want your marriage to work, keep in mind there will be ups and downs throughout the life of your marriage. There will be massive changes—some predictable and others intrusive. They hold the potential for growth, but are risky at the same time. Many marriages die because too many couples choose to ignore the inescapable fact that relationships and people change.

A wife shared the following:

Since we have been married fifty years, you can just imagine how much change that we have gone through: 3 wars, 11 Presidents, 5 recessions, going from the Model A to the moon, from country road to the information super highway. While these changes around us have been great, the personal changes that God has enacted within us through each other have been even greater. Although we often couldn't see how God was working in our lives at that time, we look back now and realize that our marriage has been a school of character development. God has used my husband in my life, and he's used me in his life to make us more like Christ. So what are the lessons that we've learned about how God uses marriage to change us? There are many. Through fifty years of marriage we've learned that differences develop us, that crises cultivate us, and that ministry melts us together.

First, God has used our differences to help us grow. There have been many, many crises that God has used to develop us and to grow us. The first one was the big, big one—the crisis of being separated as soon as we got married. Ours was a wartime romance. We met at church, dated two months, got married after three weeks of engagement, and just after two months of marriage, we didn't see each other for the next two years, for Jimmy was shipped to the South Pacific during World War II. When he returned two years later, we were total strangers, but we were married to each other!

How would you have handled that situation?

How do you handle change? How do you handle the difficult, sudden, and painful changes? You've got to be willing to face the fact that change exists—you will change, your marriage will change, your partner will want you to change, and you will want your partner to change.

I'm sure that when you marry there will be behaviors and responses on the part of your partner that you would like changed. That's normal. But keep this in mind:

> It's always a mistake to depend on your partner magically changing after marriage. Everybody changes. But basing a marriage on the hope that helpful change will just happen is a dangerous hope. Many people marry believing that intolerable conditions will improve. Those conditions do improve if there is a sufficiently strong commitment to the marriage. However, things often get worse before they get better. This time of getting worse happens because we are so reluctant to make waves—we close our feelings, confront ourselves, and face our situation. The hope that the problems will just effortlessly go away is an enticing fantasy that is hard to let go.[13]

You can impact your future partner if you're an encourager rather than a critic, a forgiver rather than a collector of hurts, an enabler rather than a reformer. I've seen so many couples where the marriage has stifled and limited one or both of the partners. But a marriage is to free each person to be all he or she can become.

Donald Harvey, author of *The Drifting Marriage* says,

> Making a commitment to marriage as an institution is not meant to be a sentencing. Its intent is to offer security and stability. All couples have conflicts. Every marriage has to make adjustments. Feeling secure in a mate's commitment to the marriage allows the opportunity for dealing with conflicts and for needed adjustments to occur. This is what makes marriage resilient.

A marriage can endure many affronts, whether from within or without, if the commitment to marriage as an institution is strong. It takes this kind of commitment for growth to occur.[14]

What is it in your life that you've made a commitment to and stuck with through the good times and the bad? What is it in your life that you've made a commitment to and discarded because of difficulties? Think of these questions in regard to a job, school, friends, promises made to others, and tithing to your church. Have you ever been more committed at times than uncommitted? If you're interested in another person (or when you do become interested), how has that person handled the commitments in his or her life? Do you know? Have you discussed it? It's necessary to discover this pattern prior to marriage.

Commitment has little to do with your feelings; it's an act of the mind and the will. Basically, you make a decision and stick with it. If you are considering marrying someone, this is the time to look at your and the other person's level of commitment.

Your decision to stick to a relationship can be what makes a marriage last. If you enter a marriage with the belief that this marriage will last "until one of us dies," your perspective is different than if you believe that divorce is an option. The key word here is *attitude*, and it's based upon God's Word.

A verse that has meant so much to me is one which I ask couples in premarital counseling to build their marriage upon: "Consider it all joy, my brethren, when you encounter various trials, knowing that the testing [or trying] of your faith produces endurance" (James 1:2,3). It's easy to read a passage like this and say, "Well, that's fine." It is another thing, however, to put it into practice.

What does the word *consider* or (*count*) actually mean? It refers to an internal attitude of the heart or the mind that allows the trial and circumstance of life to affect us adversely or beneficially. Another way James 1:2 might be translated is: "Make up your mind to regard adversity as something to welcome or be glad about."

You have the power to decide what your attitude will be. You can approach a problem and say: "That's terrible— totally upsetting. That is the last thing I wanted for my life. Why did it have to happen now? Why me?"

The other way of "considering" the same difficulty is to say: "It's not what I wanted or expected, but it's here. There are going to be some difficult times, but how can I make the best of them?"

The verb tense used in the word *consider* indicates a decisiveness of action. It's not an attitude of resignation: "Well, I'll just give up. I'm just stuck with this problem. That's the way life is." If you resign yourself, you will sit back and not put forth any effort. The verb tense actually indicates that you will have to go against your natural inclination to see the trial as a negative force. There will be some moments when you won't see it like that at all, and then you'll have to remind yourself: "No, I think there is a better way of responding to this. Lord, I really want You to help me see it from a different perspective." And then your mind will shift to a more constructive response. This often takes a lot of work on your part.

God created us with both the capacity and the freedom to determine how we will respond to those unexpected incidents that life brings our way. You may honestly wish that a certain event had never occurred. But you cannot change the fact.

My wife and I fall in the high-risk group for marriages. Our second child was profoundly mentally retarded. Having a handicapped child with any type of problem has a destructive effect on marriages in our society. About 80 percent of marriages in which there is a disabled child end in divorce. Then when our son was 22, he died. Seventy to 80 percent of couples who lose a child in death get a divorce. We learned to be survivors through the grace and comfort of God and the stability of His Word.

The attitude reflected in this verse in James means that when you encounter problems, disappointments, and difficulties in your life, why be surprised or shocked? Your partner will not be all that you expected and will disappoint you, as you will your partner. That really isn't new. The question is, How will you handle it? What can you make out of the situation? How can you grow? How could you respond differently?

If you want a healthy relationship, make it that way. Today we have a generation that reflects attitudes from the Baby Boomers and Baby Busters. There's a sense of entitlement reflected in "I deserve to have what I want and, if not, I'll bail out." There's a sense of immediate fulfillment reflected in "I don't want to wait ten years for this. I want it now." I see this quite often with couples who want to have an economic level in the first few years of their marriage that took their parents 30 years of hard work to attain. A marriage relationship will take years to develop into what you want it to become.

I like what Neil Warren has said about one of the advantages that commitment provides for a relationship.

> Commitment significantly eases the fear of abandonment. It is this fear that is central to so many persons. It is often the most potent fear of all. When we were young and unable to take care of ourselves, we worried about becoming lost in a crowd, forgotten while waiting to be picked up at school, or left alone by dying parents. Fears like these persist throughout our lives. We shudder at the very thought of abandonment.
>
> That's why a spouse's promise to remain devoted means so much. Your partner will be loyal through

every kind of circumstance. That frees you in a radical way. It allows you to be yourself at the deepest of levels, to risk and grow, to be absolutely authentic without any fear of being abandoned.[15]

Perhaps one husband's description of commitment sums it up best of all:

Commitment is dangerous. It can be exploited. If my wife takes my commitment for granted, she may rest too easily on her laurels. Perhaps commitment should be not simply to each other as we are but to the highest potentialities we can achieve together. Commitment then would be to marriage not simply as a status but as a dynamic process. Let me commit myself to a lifelong adventure, the adventure of living with this woman. The route of this adventure has been only dimly charted by those who have gone before. Because I am unique and my partner is unique, our marriage will also be unique. We commit ourselves to undertaking this adventure together, and to following wherever it may lead. Part of the excitement of marriage is not knowing in advance what either the joys or the sorrows will be. We can be sure, however, that we will be confronted with countless challenges. Commitment provides the momentum for going forward in the face of those challenges.[16]

Are you able to make such a commitment? If so, consider marriage.

Is there anything else a person needs to know before plunging into marriage?

Resolving Conflicts Successfully

It is helpful to look at the various studies that have been conducted on marriages that succeed or fail. In the book *Why Marriages Succeed or Fail*, the results show that marriages will last when a couple has the ability to resolve the conflicts that are inevitable in any relationship. Too many couples over the years have said a sign of a healthy marriage and marital happiness is having a lower level of conflict. "We never fight" is their motto. But relationships are built and strengthened by facing and reconciling differences. This is what leads to a greater level of happiness and satisfaction in marriage.

Everyone differs, however, in the way they resolve differences. The author of the book just mentioned has found there are three different styles of problem-solving that are reflected in healthy marriages. There are *validating marriages* in which couples compromise frequently. They work out their differences in a calm manner to each individual's satisfaction whenever a problem surfaces.

There are two other styles which used to be considered unhealthy patterns, but that doesn't seem to be the case reflected in *Why Marriages Succeed or Fail*. In *conflict-avoiding marriage*, couples agree to disagree but rarely confront their problems head-on. They avoid discussions they know will end up in deadlock. They focus on what they appreciate in the relationship, accentuate the positive, and accept the rest of what is unresolved. (Personally, I think there are some drawbacks to this style and the next one as well.)

The third style is the *volatile marriage* in which there are frequent and often intense disputes. Voices are raised and listening is not the best. They seem to enjoy these times, and these couples tend to be more affectionate than others as well.

So all three solve their differences in various ways.

Is there a common thread in these three varied styles that is the ingredient which brings happiness? Yes, and it's very simple. When there are *five times* as many *positive* as *negative* moments together, then your marriage is more likely to be fulfilling.[17]

What about it? If you're in a relationship now, what is the positive level compared to the negative? Going into a marriage from a position of strength is far better than with a deficit. My own feeling is if you don't learn to resolve conflicts before you marry, wait. Why proceed when you haven't learned how to develop harmony? This is a skill that anyone can learn, but the time to refine it is before the commitment is made.

Vulnerability and Intimacy

What else can you do to enhance the prospects of having a successful marriage? Following the guidelines and suggestions in this book in selecting a life partner is a beginning step. Going through extensive premarital counseling with a trained and knowledgeable counselor or minister is a must as well.

In healthy marriages there is a high degree of vulnerability and intimacy. Both persons are aware of their feelings and needs. They're willing to express what these are and how they would like them fulfilled. And they don't withdraw when conflict emerges. But keep in mind that both of you need to be able to do this. Just one doesn't carry the marriage.

Acceptance

Marriages that make it have two people who can accept imperfections and differences. They have learned how to influence one another in positive ways and bring out the best in each other. They've learned what can be changed and what cannot. Personality types and characteristics won't change; behavioral habits certainly can. What is your capability in this area?

Ability to Speak Each Other's Language

When two people plan to spend their life together, they have to be able to communicate in such a way that they connect. And since in many ways you marry a foreigner, you had better learn the other person's language. If there is one key ingredient to the complex process of communication it's this: Learn to speak your spouse's language, and the closeness and intimacy you're seeking can happen.

For example, such a simple difference as one of you being an "amplifier" when you talk and the other a "condenser" can drive a wedge between the two of you. An amplifier as used here is someone who uses several detailed, descriptive sentences in explaining something. This person wishes his or her partner would do the same. Unfortunately, they often pressure their condenser partner to open up and give a multitude of sentences. The condenser is a bottom-line sort of person who may give a two-sentence response, but often one line is sufficient. This person would like his or her partner to do the same. They can tune out quite readily when their spouse amplifies. If each would adapt their natural style to their spouse's style when they talk, each would respond better. We'll talk more about this in another chapter.

In a counseling session one day a man said, "I'd like to find a woman that I could understand and get along with as well as I get along with my male friends, but it's impossible." I said, "No, it's not. It's very possible if you are willing to become flexible, realize that you and a woman are aliens, that you need to learn about male-female cultural differences, and learn to see them as a learning challenge that can enrich your life rather than view them as a pain in the neck. If you do that, you'll get along!"

There are many factors which contribute to our unique way of communication, including personality, gender, and learning style. When you learn and implement what you have learned, the intimacy in your relationship will develop. (For complete information on

personality types, gender differences, and help in learning how to speak one another's language, see chapters
4-9 in *How to Change Your Spouse Without Ruining Your
Marriage* by this author and Gary Oliver, Servant Publishers).

Couples where both people are secure in who they
are and aren't looking for their partner to be the solution
to their self-identity or esteem problems are much hap-
pier in their relationship. The other person's calling is
not to be a current substitute for what was lacking in
your life or for what was missing between you and a
parent when you were growing up. Keep in mind that
you can't be happily married to another person unless
you're happily married to yourself. Your partner is not
responsible for making you feel good about yourself or
for giving you an identity. That you receive from your
relationship with Jesus Christ.

Spiritual Intimacy

There is one final ingredient which will stabilize a
marriage and open the doors for the depth of intimacy
that couples are seeking. Spiritual intimacy is that ele-
ment of marriage in which the couple's heart, mind, and
soul are open to the Lord and one another. It means you
have similar beliefs which are important to you, including a personal relationship with Jesus Christ. It also
means you have the freedom to share your feelings and
thoughts of where you are spiritually. You share new
insights with one another that you have learned from
Scripture or a resource you're reading. You pray for and
with each other and worship together. You feel comfortable and close in relating spiritually and endeavor to
make Jesus Christ the Lord of your life and your relationship. I said relationship, rather than marriage, because
this dimension of intimacy needs to be part and parcel of
the development of the growth of your relationship. It

won't just happen after you marry. When it's intertwined with the developing of your love relationship as you consider marriage, it becomes an integral and natural part of your relationship.

A Marriage Definition

There are so many other elements that could be mentioned about making a marriage work. Let me sum it up with a definition of marriage that I've been working on for the past 20 years. It states what a marriage is, what it can be, and what it takes for it to be all you want it to be: "A Christian marriage is a total commitment of two people to the person of Jesus Christ and to one another. It is a commitment in which there is no holding back of anything. Marriage is a pledge of mutual fidelity in all areas. It is a partnership of mutual subordination and servanthood."

A Christian marriage is similar to a solvent, a freeing up of the man and woman to be themselves and become all that God intends for them to become. Marriage is a refining process that God will use to have us develop into the man or woman He wants us to become.

Well, is marriage something you want? If so, it may take more than you realize. Keep this last thought in mind as you read on:

> True success is never an easy achievement. Happy and fulfilling marriages are products of extreme effort. They are desired, sought after, fought for, and planned. They never *just* happen. Couples frequently complain to me how their marriage *just* fell apart. All of a sudden, they just fell out of love . . . just lost interest in a husband . . . just fell in love with another person or career. If experience has taught me anything, it is this: Nothing *just* happens . . . whether good or bad.

Healthy marriages follow a road . . . a road that is planned. You do not have to plan to fail. That can be accomplished without planning . . . and usually is. But you DO have to plan to succeed.[18]

"I'm Afraid of a Relationship"

Remember when you saw someone of the opposite sex you thought was super? Was it junior high? Maybe it was high school or college. Every time you saw him or her your heart started racing and your stomach went "twang." You wanted to meet this person. You wanted a date. But how?

You began to plan.

You asked your friends about this great person. You found out their class schedule and the route they took to get there, and you just happened to start walking that way. Or you found out where they worked, and you went in and ordered a Big Mac and fries three times a day to see them. But how could you possibly get up the nerve to ask for a date or let it be known that you were available? Never! When it came to that, you froze. Your thoughts wouldn't work with your mouth. You were frozen with fear. What if they said no? What if they laughed at you? What if they told everyone else and they all laughed at you? What if . . . what if . . . the turmoil of an adolescent. You were so glad when it was over. But you just *thought* it was over. Those in their twenties, thirties, and upwards can experience the same kind of turmoil. It's called fear.

Many single people live in a self-imposed prison of fear. I have seen numerous people who have found the "right" person, but are immobilized from taking that important step of marriage because of fear. Some have allowed fear to become the dictator of their life.

We all have a sense of fear when pursuing a new relationship. Why? Because there are risks involved. You may have a fear of being alone the rest of your life, but as you move toward a lasting relationship you bump into other fears. These can include the fear of closeness, fear of dependence, fear of losing independence, fear of rejection, fear of commitment, fear of failure, fear of making a mistake, and the list continues. One woman said, "I guess I'm afraid that if I marry I'll discover some things about myself that I never knew before and won't like!"

The unspoken concern of many singles was written years ago by John Powell: "I'm afraid to tell you who I am because you might not like who I am and that's all I've got." Perhaps the common denominator in the various fears is the fear of pain. We become very skillful in developing excuses. Many of us learn to put on some form of a mask to keep that lost vestige of distance in place. Some people use denial; others use work. Some become a clown, and others use their intellect.

What fear about relationships lives within you at the present time? Is it a normal level of fear or is it dominating your life? We weren't created to be driven by fear but rather to be drawn ahead in life by hope. How would you complete this statement: "What I fear most in a relationship is . . ."?

Fear of Commitment

Let's consider one fear that is at the core of a long-term

marriage—commitment. This fear appears to be the opposite of one most of us experience—the fear of rejection. Some individuals are afraid they may be too successful. They see commitment carrying with it the loss of freedom, too many responsibilities, and as one man voiced it, "What if I see someone better who comes along after I'm married? Then I'm stuck!" or "What if the person I marry isn't what I thought they would be? Then what? I don't want to make a mistake."

Blaine Smith suggests four levels at which the fear of commitment commonly occurs. Perhaps you've witnessed or experienced this in some way. Some people make such a dramatic, hasty exit from a growing relationship it reminds you of a prison break. The pressure of the thought of confinement pushes them into a panicky act which shows little or no regard for the feelings of the other person.

Other people manifest their fear through an on-again, off-again type of relationship. When the commitment is off, they feel comfortable with the relationship again. But as it moves toward commitment, the doubts once again begin to dominate their mind and soon they retreat.

Some people feel a sense of continuing ambivalence because their fear of commitment matches their level of desire for marriage. The relationship is serious, but the discussion about marriage usually falls in the realm of a "possibility." A decision is always just out of reach. The word *eventually* keeps the couple involved, but if the relationship goes beyond a certain level, the person becomes frozen by fear. What is unfortunate is that this kind of a relationship can go on for years.

The last level is normal apprehension. In this situation, the desire for marriage overrides the fear of commitment. This fear can help you take a hard and clear look at the relationship and take what may be positive growth steps.[19]

When it comes down to making a relationship permanent through commitment, the subtle "what if" germ begins to invade our minds. "What if I'm attracted to someone else after I'm married?" "What if this isn't God's will for my life?" "What if I commit myself and the relationship fails?" "What if I commit myself and I get hurt?" Endless "what if" questions keep many couples from the commitment and intimacy that help make a marriage strong.

Tim Timmons and Charlie Hedges talk about three of the major fears of commitment. First, there is the fear of giving love without receiving love in return. We all want to receive love in the same measure we give it. And in a marriage, giving without receiving is very painful.

Second, the fear of being used and taken advantage of is an inhibitor to commitment, especially after one partner gives personal information about himself.

Third, one of the most paralyzing fears preventing commitment is desertion. Desertion is the ultimate form of rejection. Anyone who has been jilted in the past always has the fear of desertion lurking in the back of his mind, blocking future commitments.[20] Have you found yourself described yet?

If you are experiencing the fear of commitment, make a list of all those items you feel you will be giving up or losing when you marry. Evaluate them. Will you really be giving them up completely? Spend time grieving over what you will lose. Say good-bye to them, and then say hello to all those things you will be gaining.

Fear of Rejection

The fear of rejection keeps us in a protective, cautious state. It hurts, but sometimes we let it hurt too much.

Kay was a very sensitive person who had experienced rejection in her childhood home and in some of her relationships with men. As we talked together, she shared the extent of her feelings:

> I don't like the way I am. I know I'm overly sensitive. When I made the appointment with you, I even wondered if you would accept me as a client. Then when I arrived this morning and you were three minutes late for my appointment, those old feelings of rejection began to climb to the surface. It wasn't you but my own sensitivity. I feel that way whenever someone changes plans with me or disagrees with what I think or want. Anytime someone doesn't go along with what I want, I begin to feel rejected. And then I get angry inside.
>
> When I am dating a man and I care for him, I'm even more sensitive to any sign of rejection. But when I feel rejected, I come on too strong and demand love and acceptance in some way. And that chases him right out the door! When that happens, I feel terrible. And I know I caused the rejection. But I don't know what to do!
>
> That's not the only way I respond to my fear of rejection. Sometimes I feel real inhibited with a man, so I withdraw. I'm afraid of exposing my true self and being rejected. But my withdrawal also brings on rejection because he sees me as a real dud. I can't let him know that I care for him and crave his attention and acceptance. So I don't get it. And once again, I get mad! It's almost like I'm caught in a vicious cycle. But I don't know how to get out of it!

Kay was right. It easily becomes a vicious cycle, and it's very common. If you live with the fear of rejection, you expect it. It elevates your need for acceptance by other people. But you tend to behave in a way that hinders others from accepting you. I see it happening in one of two ways. Either people are so closed, restrained, or timid that you would have to use a battering ram to get through. Or they become so demanding and controlling that they drive that special person right out of their life. With either choice, rejection will be the outcome, and their fear becomes a self-fulfilling prophecy.

If you experience rejection, you feel hurt. Often that turns into anger. But if you express your anger, what happens? Rejection. So the anger is stuffed, which feeds the fear, and soon the pattern is repeated. This keeps a relationship from going anywhere.

Some of us are especially sensitive to any hint of rejection. And because of this tendency, rejection is seen in statements and actions when it isn't even there. We live with the ghosts of rejection. Every rejection we've experienced in the past causes us to be overly sensitive to what's happening in the present. The pain of previous rejections stays with us and contaminates current relationships. Unfortunately, some people were treated as unacceptable, unwanted burdens when they were young. Feelings of rejection in childhood can result from the presence of derogatory statements or the absence of physical or verbal affirmation. When a person is rejected as a child, he is more sensitive to hurt as an adult.

Phil grew up in a home where everybody was work-oriented and very busy. There was no emotional closeness, physical affection, or interest shown to the children. His parents were busy with their own lives and showed very little interest in his accomplishments at school. In his teen years, Phil began to wonder why his family wasn't close to him and why no one took much interest in him. He wondered what it was about him that his parents didn't like. They weren't mean or abusive to him. They were polite and courteous, but sterile in their responses. Phil said:

I could never understand why they were so distant. We were together as a family, but it felt like we were miles apart. And then I began to wonder if there was something wrong with me. I felt like I was a burden even though they always provided for me. They never said I was a burden—but I felt that way.

Because of my childhood experience, I've always been fairly cautious about getting close to someone. Maybe there is something wrong with me, and I just can't see it. Sometimes I have daydreams and night dreams about others rejecting me. In my relationships with women, I'm very cautious about getting involved. I'm afraid they will do what my parents did—ignore me. To me, being ignored hurts the same as someone telling me, "You stink. You're no good. I don't like you, and I don't want you." My folks never said those words exactly, but their actions made me feel as though they had.

If I meet a woman I'm interested in, I begin to wonder, "Will she really like me or want me?" I would rather wait for a woman to show an interest in me and pursue me. That's safer. I don't like to pursue them because if they turn me down...

But let's face it. You will experience rejection as you look for a life partner. Even in a lasting relationship you will experience rejections from time to time. And the more we are addicted to approval, the greater our fear of rejection. But rejection is not the end of the world, even with its accompanying pain. Too often when the rejection comes the negative-thinking bent of our mind kicks into play and we begin to say, "There must be something wrong with me. I'm not 'this or that' or I must be too... " and we become our best (or worst) critic.

Keep this thought in mind. When you are rejected, is the person who is doing the rejecting making a statement about you or making more of a statement about himself or herself? Is it really a problem within you or is it their problem? What would happen if you would begin to assume this in place of the negative perspective about yourself? Rejection may be unpleasant, but it doesn't have to destroy your self-esteem and self-confidence. You will survive.

If you live with the fear of rejection, you may be operating with a selective memory that needs to be channeled in a new direction. Perhaps you overemphasize the times you've experienced rejection, rather than focusing on all the times of acceptance. Could it be that you reject yourself in some ways? The more we make rejecting, negative statements about ourselves, the more we see other people doing the same. Could that be the case now? Sometimes this tendency causes us to respond to others in such a way that they may reject us. We set ourselves up.

If rejection occurs, there are some things you can do. Keep in mind that when someone does respond to you in a rejecting manner, it may be that he or she is having a bad day. Or perhaps that person has misinterpreted your response. Or they could be a highly critical, hurting person. It may be somebody else's problem. It could also be that no one is at fault; the incident that made you feel rejected just happened for some unexplained reason. Being rejected doesn't necessarily mean you have done or said something wrong. It doesn't mean you're defective.

If you make a mistake that could cause rejection, don't anticipate being rejected ahead of time. Balance your feelings by focusing on the numerous times you were successful. See your small mistake in the context of the positive side of your life. Putting this in writing will have a greater impact upon you than just thinking about it.

Criticism and rejection from a special person can upset you only to the extent that you believe the response of the other person. You can let it linger and destroy you, or you can move ahead. Yes, rejection hurts, and it's uncomfortable. But avoid the hippopotamus response—don't wallow in your feelings of rejection. Refuse to believe that one rejection will lead to others or that your world is falling apart. Instead, take charge of the situation when it occurs, and turn the negative into a positive by responding to it with courage. If the criticism has validity, consider that as well.

When you are rejected, keep in mind that the other person has neither the right nor the ability to judge your value and worth as a person. Don't allow the negative responses to determine your value. People are not experts on your worth; God is. I like what Dr. David Burns says about approval and disapproval:

> It's a fact that approval *feels* good. There's nothing wrong with that: it's natural and healthy. It is also a fact that disapproval and rejection usually taste bitter and unpleasant. This is human and understandable. But you are swimming in deep, turbulent waters if you continue to believe that approval and disapproval are the proper and ultimate yardsticks with which to measure your worth.[21]

When you live with the fear of rejection, you live with assumptions based on emotions. Your emotions tell you what to believe about events and relationships. They tell you that you will be rejected and that you *are* rejected. Counter these feelings with actual facts. Unless you behave in a way that causes you to be rejected, most of the time you won't be rejected. But when you are rejected, don't assume that you're at fault.

I have felt rejection. I have felt the rejection of someone not liking my speaking, my writing, or my counseling. I have had my ideas rejected, and I have been personally rejected by other people. I experienced rejections during my dating years. I don't like it. In fact, it's so uncomfortable to feel rejected, I've often wondered why anyone would want to live with the *fear* of rejection.[22]

Fear of Intimacy

Another fear which keeps us from moving into marriage is the closeness that intimacy brings, especially emotional closeness. This is ironic because intimacy eliminates the pain of loneliness. As one man said, "I want it, but the time payments are too high."

As I've counseled singles over the years, I've discovered that one of the reasons for avoiding emotional closeness is low self-esteem. If you constantly criticize yourself, you will probably fear that other people will follow your example and criticize you, too. As one woman said, "When a man starts getting close, I run. I just know he's going to become critical of me. I'm enough of a critic of myself. I don't need his criticism." And the fear of seeing her own criticism come through another person keeps her blocked. If you want to be vulnerable to another person and experience love and closeness, you have to accept and love yourself. And it's possible because of who God is and how He sees us.

It is rare to find a man who doesn't have some struggles with intimacy. Men love the benefits of intimacy, but often they are not committed to the work intimacy entails. Though few of them will admit it, most men fear intimacy, and this fear is reflected in the way they interact with their wives, families, and friends.

Why do men avoid intimacy? Listen to a few of their responses, which reflect rationalizations rather than actual reasons:

"That's just the way men are. We aren't intimate the way women are. They may not like it, but that's just the way it is for us men."

"We don't know any differently. It's good enough for us."

"If you open up and share your feelings, others will take advantage of you. It's just not safe. It comes back to haunt you."

"You can't be macho and vulnerable at the same time. It just doesn't work, and I wouldn't know how to learn anyway."

"Very honestly, I just don't know how to be emotionally intimate. I don't have the words, the vocabulary to describe what women want to hear. And when I try I sound like a jerk. I want to be a success, not a failure. So I won't try."

"The main reason I can't be intimate is that when I try, my wife is the judge of whether or not I've shared a true feeling. I really *do* try to open up and get as close as she asks. But there's got to be a list of rules about feelings and closeness somewhere that only women know. From her perspective, I never get it right. So why try?"

"I don't know whether or not I'm comfortable telling her everything. If I did something to make her mad, she'd use it against me. She's shared some things with her friends that I thought were only between the two of us. That hurt. I don't think women use good judgment when private discussions are concerned."

A major concern for men about intimacy with women is trust. Some men have had bad experiences after opening themselves up to the women in their lives. *Whom* can

they trust? Many men believe women perceive information differently, and they share in public what men see as
only personal.

Another concern for men has its roots in the issue of
control. When a man shares his personal thoughts and
feelings in order to draw close to someone, he is poten-
tially giving that person influence over him. That individual can use the information shared either *for* his welfare or *against* his welfare. It's risky.[23]

Women struggle with the fear of intimacy as well.
There are several reasons why a woman might fear an
intimate relationship. One we've already talked about—
the pain of rejection. This issue seems to be at the core of
so many fears. Irene was a young divorcée who was
attempting to make the adjustment back into single life.
She complained to me one day:

> I poured myself into that relationship for four
> years. I held nothing back, thinking my openness
> would make it work. It didn't. I felt abandoned
> when he walked out of my life. I gave and he took.
> Then I got left behind. Why care that much? Why
> get that close? The closer you get, the more it hurts
> when they leave you. I was very close to my dad,
> and when he died at age forty-three it was like part
> of me was dead, too. And that happened just a year
> before Jim said "so long." If you love them too
> much, they will kill you emotionally when they
> leave. Never again.

Yes, it does hurt when intimate relationships fall
apart. But when there is *no* intimacy and closeness in a
relationship, there is an *even greater chance* of a relationship dissolving! When you insulate yourself against
other people, you tend to bring about that which you fear
the most—abandonment. The courage to run the risk of

intimacy can bring tremendous fulfillment in life for both men and women. Often we can predict in premarital counseling the potential for the lack of intimacy developing in a relationship. It's the key factor in the bonding process, and when you have an ingredient missing, bonding won't happen.

Women also struggle with the fear of losing their identity in an intimate relationship with a man. Even though women tend to encourage and be more comfortable with intimacy than men, some women fear losing their sense of independence and autonomy if they get too close to their men. I've seen this fear happen all too much.

We all need our own space, our privacy, and our separateness. That's normal. But some women are afraid a man's demands for closeness and sharing may become too energy-draining for them. They fear their men may begin to invade their lives too much. And in some cases, if a man is vulnerable and discloses his deepest feelings, both positive and negative, she fears he might be weak and unable to give her the care she desires.

Steps to Overcoming Fear

What can you do about your fears? The initial step is facing and accepting the fact that fear may be ruling your life in some way. And if so, identify what the fears are. List them, and then evaluate each on a scale of 0 to 10 to discover the intensity. A 0 indicates no fear, 5 is average, and 10 is very intense. Ask yourself the question, "What am I doing to keep this fear alive in my life?" You may be surprised at the answer. Talk about your fear with a trusted friend who can assist you. List the results of living by fear or becoming a risk-taker. Face your fear by doing the thing of which you are afraid. This breaks the power of fear. Look to God's Word for guidance, wisdom, and control of your fears. One of my favorite passages is Psalm 37. It begins, "Do not fret," and those words are repeated later in the chapter. The dictionary defines *fret* as "to eat away, gnaw, gall, vex, worry, agitate, wear away."

Whenever I hear this word, I'm reminded of the scene I see each year when I hike along the Snake River in the Grand Teton National Park in Wyoming. Families of beavers live along the riverbanks, and often I see trees that are at various stages of being gnawed to the ground. Some trees have slight rings around their necks where the beavers have just started to chew. Other trees have several inches of bark eaten away, and some have already fallen to the ground because the beavers have gnawed through the trunks. Worry and fear have the same effect on us. They will gradually eat away at us until they destroy us. And they will keep us from having the love we want in a relationship.

In addition to telling us not to fret, Psalm 37 gives us positive substitutes for worry. First, it says, "Trust (lean on, rely on, and be confident) in the Lord" (verse 3, AMP). Trust is a matter of not attempting to live an independent life or to cope with difficulties alone. It means going to a greater source for strength.

Second, verse 4 says, "Delight yourself also in the Lord" (AMP). To delight means to rejoice in God and what He has done for us. Let God supply the joy of your life.

Third, verse 5 says, "Commit your way to the Lord" (AMP). Commitment is a definite act of the will, and it involves releasing your worries and anxieties to the Lord.

And fourth, we are to "rest in the Lord; wait for Him" (verse 7, AMP). This means to submit in silence to what He ordains but to be ready and expectant for what He is going to do in your life.

Have you ever considered the question, "Why did God put so many 'fear nots' in the Bible when He knows we tend to be fearful creatures?" God's "fear nots" are just another way He has provided for you. God doesn't want your life to be a chore. Fear makes it that. God doesn't want you to be driven by fear but by hope. And He gives you the hope you need when He says, "Fear not."

You can be a free person without compromising who you are out of fear of others. Life is a risk, but risks give you a great opportunity to learn to live by faith. Fear will no longer be the dominating force in your life if you refuse to let it be. Your imagination is one of God's greatest gifts to you. Use it! Your imagination can generate fear, or it can be a vehicle for bringing God's peace and calm into your life. Isaiah the prophet said, "Thou dost keep him in perfect peace, whose mind is stayed on thee" (Isaiah 26:3, RSV). If marriage is part of your dream, don't let fear become your life's companion rather than a person. If remaining single is your choice, let it be because it is God's calling for you rather than because you are afraid.

If You Haven't Recovered—Wait!

*I*t's been three years since the breakup. Wouldn't you think that by now I could move into a new relationship without being haunted by a ghost? I seem to cripple every new relationship because of what happened in the last one. I know I was hurt, but when does it go away for good!? I think I'm OK, but then I become emotionally involved with someone and the hurt and anger come rushing back. And guess who I dump it on!"

It's tough to recover from a broken relationship. When you're in love with a person who loves you back, it's wonderful. But when they don't, it's like the end of the world for some people. There are times when you wonder, Will I ever heal? It could be a long-term relationship, an engagement, or a marriage that ended. They're all filled with pain, especially if you're the one rejected. And it may never go away completely if you are a parent. You will always be linked through your children to that individual in some way for the rest of your life.

When a relationship dissolves, you are facing a death—the death of dreams, hopes, aspirations, as well as what you actually had in the relationship itself. You're losing a history and a part of your life. Even if you were the person who terminated the relationship because you no longer cared for the person or the relationship, there is still a death, although it may be mingled with relief.

In all but a few breakups each person will play a different role. One is the rejector and the other the rejectee. A rejector can suffer just as much as the rejectee. That may sound odd to you, but it's not so much the role you played, but who has the most emotional investment in the relationship. That person has the most to lose, regardless of the way the relationship comes apart. Do women hurt more in a breakup than men? Not necessarily. They hurt differently, just like they tend to grieve differently.

Men and women tend to view relationships differently. For example, men don't usually define self-esteem by the success or failure of a relationship, whereas women tend to put more emphasis on the quality of relationships. Women may tend to hurt longer and deeper as well as second-guess themselves. They may ask, "Where did I go wrong?"

Why is this chapter important to you if you are already seeking another person? You cannot move into a new, healthy, and possibly permanent relationship if you still have emotional energy tied up in the last relationship.

You may think you've recovered and perhaps you have . . . and then again, maybe you haven't. Some individuals haven't recovered, but aren't aware of it until they're in the midst of a new relationship. Then it hits them. And the unexpectedness of it turns their life upside down. They discover they haven't fully let go.

Three Roles in Recovery

When a relationship dissolves there are actually three different roles for the participants. In your past relationships, you could have experienced all three. One role is called the "willing rejector." In this position you have divorced yourself emotionally and intellectually from the other person, whether you are in a marriage or a dating relationship. It could have occurred slowly like a subtle emotion or suddenly like a volcano erupting. When you break off the relationship, your behavior is now consistent with your thoughts. Because you are in charge of what is happening, your recovery might be more rapid than if you were the rejectee. You're the one who has had more time to prepare yourself for this decision and act. Your greatest pain and even guilt may be the pain your ex is experiencing.

Some people end up being "unwilling rejectors." When this occurs, your pain and discomfort can be the same as that of the rejectee. Some have said, "This is crazy. I feel like a villain and a victim at the same time. How did this happen?" It's true. You can end up feeling torn apart. You are the one ending the relationship, and this accounts for your feeling like a villain. But if you still love the person, you feel victimized as well. It's as though your relief over ending the relationship is over-shadowed by the emotional pain you experience.

Sometimes what prompts you to take the step of breaking up is in one way or another already feeling rejected by the other party. Your partner or spouse may be involved with someone else while still with you or may be consumed by work and sports. Sometimes partners have affairs with things and activities rather than with another person. Sometimes your act of rejecting the person is an act of trying to wake them up so the relationship can be saved. I've seen this happen when the partner was consumed by work, overly involved with their family of origin, involved in drugs, alcoholism, pornography, etc.

The difficulty of being an "unwilling rejector" is the dual feeling of hoping it's over to escape the pain, but also hoping it will work. You experience blame and grief at the same time or alternate back and forth. This hampers decision-making. It's difficult to reconcile a victim and villain when you are both of them. Sometimes you end up returning to the person for a while, hoping that what prompted you to leave no longer exists. I have seen some partners return and leave, return and leave, several times over a period of several years, but frequently the relationship doesn't work out. I have seen a number of marital separations work, though, because there is a greater emotional investment in a marriage than a dating relationship. There is more to lose if it were to dissolve.

The classic victim in a relationship breakup is really the "rejectee," since they have no control over what is happening. Sometimes you have indications that this may be going to happen, and you're worried about it. Or you could be denying the obvious signs. Yet again, you could be oblivious, and it comes as a major shock. An acquaintance of mine told me his wife suggested they go out to dinner one evening, and while they were sitting there eating, his wife informed him in a very factual way that their 32-year marriage was over and she was filing for divorce the next morning. This came as a complete shock to him, since there were no indications of difficulties or her dissatisfaction. He was crushed emotionally and financially for the next several years. It was a total shock and total rejection. The greater the level of unawareness and suddenness of any breakup, the greater the shock and pain. Not only do you lose the person you still care about, you lose a piece of yourself, your self-worth.[24]

Which one of the three have you tended to be over the years: a willing rejector, an unwilling rejector, or the rejectee? Is there a pattern, and if so, what does this tell you about your relationships? Which one have you been recently? On a scale of 0 to 10, where are you now in your recovery?

How Long Does the Pain Last?

"Norm, how long? How long is this pain going to last? How long is it going to take for me to recover? When will the thoughts, the feelings, the memories go away enough that I can go on with my life?" I hear this question frequently, because I work with many people who are experiencing grief in some way over the loss of a relationship. I'm not sure I can give you an exact answer, because the estimates vary. We do know, for example, when you lose a close loved one in what is called a "normal" death, the average length of time for recovery is about two years. With an accidental death, it's three years. The authors of *Letting Go*, a book dealing with recovering from a broken heart, feel (based on interviews with those who suffer from depression, feelings of inadequacy, and loss of self-esteem) the average time it took for normal functioning to return and the absence of haunting memories was usually half the time the relationship existed. That would mean a four-year marriage or relationship would take two years to recover from and a 12-year marriage or relationship, six years of recovery. I'm not sure that this should be used as a guideline, since every relationship, every person, and every situation varies. It may be accurate if the person didn't engage in their grief work and move toward recovery. The authors also state that by following the principles suggested, the symptoms mentioned will leave in three months.[25]

Two other authors have described the state you feel during a breakup as "love shock" which is basically a mixture of numbness, disorientation, emptiness, and a jumble of numerous feelings which churn about. It is similar to a crisis reaction or grieving over any kind of loss. They suggest it takes most people about a year to complete their "love shock" experience, but it's not unusual for it to take longer.[26]

I think a rule of thumb to follow is, the more you have learned to cope with crisis and the more knowledgeable you are about the losses of life and grief, the better you will be able to recover.

What Happens When It's Over?

When a close relationship ends, a part of you wants to try again with a new relationship. But another part of you says, "Forget it! It isn't worth the risk!" You are afraid the past will recur and your new relationship will also end in a painful breakup. Or you are afraid you will always feel the loss and pain of your previous breakup and never be able to reach out and love again. This fear is intensified whenever you relive the breakup. Every time you relive the experience in your memory, the emotional sledgehammer crashes down on you again. I have even heard people say they thought they were going crazy during this phase.

The fear of reliving the past paralyzes the normal process of building a new relationship. This fear creates a hesitancy to invest energy, love, and transparency in a new love interest. You ask, "What if this happens again?" Many people who are afraid to move ahead in a new relationship are also afraid to remain behind without anyone to love. But when you jump into a relationship too soon, you contaminate it and avoid dealing with the last one. You feel trapped between the fear of loving again and the fear of never being loved again. It seems to be more intense when you are the rejected person in a divorce.

There are additional emotions that feed the fear of loving again. One of them is guilt—the feeling that you have failed yourself, your ideals, your Lord, or the other person, especially if there was sexual involvement and/or living together. Sometimes you feel "I wasted four years of my life!" This guilt may exist whether you were the *rejected* person or the *rejecting* person. Unresolved guilt damages self-esteem, and low self-esteem produces greater fear. If you feel guilty about a broken relationship, it is important to identify whether the feelings are based on reality (such as breaking a commitment or acting irresponsibly toward the other person) or imagination (taking the blame for something that was not really your responsibility). I've heard of many painful aftermaths of breakups. One girl's fiancé broke up with her and married her sister. How do you imagine she felt? Another young woman was dating a 50-year-old man who was crazy about her. One day he introduced her to his 28-year-old son. Five weeks later, she and the son were married.

When breakups occur, you long for the relationship you once had. For some, this longing becomes an obsession dominating every waking moment. Nothing has any meaning until that relationship is restored. There are some who become addicted to a person. We call this obsessive love. This is the belief that this one and only one magic person can meet one's needs. To offset the pain, some people begin binging with one-night stands or eating like food is going to be rationed in the future. Restoration of the relationship exactly as it was happens very infrequently. The feeling of being out of control is particularly devastating, since there is nothing you can do. You can beg, plead, offer bribes, threaten suicide, and so on, all to no avail. Nothing seems to work, nothing will work, and nothing does work. You feel abandoned, forsaken, betrayed, and all alone.

Stages of Recovery

Like the grief we experience when a person dies, the stages you will go through to recover from a lost relationship are predictable. These stages constitute the normal and healthy process of recovery. If the healing is complete, you will have some emotional scars but no open wounds. I have talked to some people who still had oozing wounds from a relationship for over 15 years. That's sad. If you don't grieve, you won't be complete. You have to allow the relationship to die, to be over. If you don't, you're carrying around a corpse with you, and in time it begins to stink.

Please keep in mind that the stages identified here vary in their length and intensity, depending upon the duration and strength of the relationship. When the breakup is not your doing or desire, the result is even more intense.

There are usually six stages you will go through when a love relationship falls apart. Your pain will be the greatest during the first three stages. You can count on that. As you move through each stage, the intensity of your pain will diminish, but it can come roaring back when you least expect it. The further along the path you proceed, the less fear you will experience. The worst thing to have happen is to get stuck in a stage and not complete the process.

Some of these stages overlap, and you may move back and forth between them for a while. This is quite normal. It is a part of the healing process. So when you move into the next stage, don't be thrown when the previous one resurfaces.

Stage One: Shock. When you first lose a love relationship, you feel dumbfounded and overwhelmed by shock. We call this the impact stage in a crisis. Even when the breakup or divorce has been anticipated, the reality of it has a unique effect. Often there is a sense of numbness.

Some people are unable to carry on their day-to-day activities; even eating and sleeping are chores. You live by your feelings at this stage.

Whether or not you can identify it, you will experience an intense fear of being alone or of being abandoned forever. But you need to experience these feelings in order to move through the healing process. At this stage, you need to have other people around you, whether or not you feel like having them around. Just the presence of other people can help ease the fear of loneliness.

Stage Two: Grief. The grief stage may be extensive, because it includes mourning the loss of what you shared together and what you *could have* shared together. During this time, anger may be experienced, and in some ways needs to be expressed. You may be angry at yourself, at God, and at people who don't understand your grief. You may become depressed about the broken relationship and the hopelessness of relationships in the future. You may tend to see all men or all women from this same perspective. In order to grieve and move ahead, you have to accept the fact that the relationship is over. You realize your loved one is gone, and now you feel empty. Perhaps it's best expressed in an older song by Karen and Richard Carpenter:

Good-bye to Love

There are no tomorrows for this heart of mine.
Surely time will lose these bitter mem'ries
And I'll find that there is someone to believe in
And to live for, something I could live for.[27]

When the ended relationship is a divorce, this is the time when certain "divorce myths" rear their heads. The first is, "Nobody understands." It is the feeling that your situation is so unique and unusual, it is inconceivable to think anyone else could understand. It is important to realize that those who have gone through this do understand every aspect of it. They understand the feelings of abandonment, self-blame, other-blame, anger, guilt, the knife-like anguish and pain.

"I am going to die" is a predominant feeling. Everything is seen through this filter. But as one person described it, "Do I hurt a great deal at this time? Yes. Do I wish I were dead? Yes. Do I wish I could die? No."[28]

Many people experience mild paranoia. Statements like, "Everyone is talking about me," "I'm the subject of their conversations," "I can tell they're avoiding me," and "No one wants to be around me," are frequently made. Unfortunately, the person often believes these statements, and worse yet, in some narrow, unloving churches, they are sometimes true. Emotional sensitivity is heightened at this time, and becoming self-conscious is common.

Other common myths of divorced people are, "Everybody hates me," "God hates me," and "He is so displeased with me." These thoughts are just not true. God hates the act of divorce, but He does not hate the divorced person. When people respond to you differently, it is not because of a defect in you. They could be self-conscious because they don't know what to say. After all, who has ever given us guidelines on how to respond when someone goes through a broken relationship![29]

In addition to these thoughts, an entire range of symptoms may begin to reside in you. Another type of obsessional thinking begins to take you prisoner. It is a sign of hanging on to the relationship.

1. You arrange "accidental meetings" with the other person.

2. Your thought life is consumed by the other person.

3. You listen for the telephone and run for it when it rings.

4. You listen to sad songs and think they are about you and the one you lost.

5. You think you see your former love or his or her car everywhere.

6. You want to contact the person, but you are afraid of rejection.

7. You follow people or cars thinking it is the person you lost.

8. You spend a great amount of time thinking about the person, devising plans of what to say or how to get him or her back, or wondering if what he said when you were together was untrue.

9. You just know that this relationship was the best one you could ever have. Some even send unwanted and unwelcome gifts, phone them continuously, drive by their home or work place, show up unannounced or even engage in stalking them! Unfortunately, some go one step further and give up the crusade to win them back and turn to revenge. Rage has replaced love.[30]

What other thoughts do you have? Perhaps it would help to make a list of them and take steps to put them to rest.[31]

Thought-stopping is a necessary step so that reality has a chance to gain a foothold in your life once again. If you find yourself in this defeating lifestyle, you will need to shut off your obsessive thoughts, obsessive feelings, and obsessive behaviors. If you slow one down, the others will follow. This means no calling, showing up, gifts, letters, etc.

When you have thoughts that continue to return again and again, there is hope. They *can* be evicted from your life. There are two specific steps to take. First, pray out loud, sharing your concern, and describe specifically what you want God to do with these thoughts. Second, read aloud the following passages, which talk about how we can control our thought-life: Isaiah 26:3; Ephesians 4:23; Colossians 3:1,2; 2 Corinthians 10:5; Philippians 4:6-9.

Another way to handle these thoughts is a bit wild. Identify one of the most persistent or upsetting thoughts, the one that pops into your head more frequently than any of the others. Select a time when you are fairly calm. Say the statement or statements out loud without crying or becoming angry, if you can. If you can't, that's all right. In time, you will be able to do this. When you say the last word of the statement (such as, "How could she have been so deceptive and *unfair*?"), slam a book or ruler loudly on a table or just clap your hands. Repeat the sentence and move the noise back one word each time you repeat the bothersome thought. In time, this thought will be interrupted before it has a chance to begin. And as this happens, thank God for taking this thought from your life.[32]

Stage Three: Blame. Feelings of blame, accompanied by anger, may be held toward your former spouse, fiancée, or dating partner—or even toward yourself. Your behavior during this stage may surprise you as you attempt to rid yourself of these feelings. Your actions may not seem to fit your past patterns. You may engage in compulsive behaviors such as shopping or eating binges, alcohol abuse, or even promiscuity. It is not unusual for people to make poor decisions at this stage. Fears of rejection, isolation, or personal inadequacy prompt some people to act contrary to their own value systems.

Fred was a 35-year-old whose wife divorced him to marry her employer. He was devastated by the divorce, but gradually he began to date again. However, he was quite unsuccessful in his new relationships.

One day Fred explained:

> I guess I'm still angry at Irene for leaving me. But there's no way I can make her pay for what she did to me, and I can't take my anger out on her. So that's probably why these new relationships aren't working out. I like the women I date, but I don't treat them well. I get angry at them, and I'm often rude. That's just not me! I guess I'm trying to get back at my wife by taking my anger out on these other women. And that isn't good for them or for me. I guess I try to hurt them first, because I'm afraid they may hurt me the way my wife did. And I don't ever want to be hurt like that again!

Fortunately, Fred had the insight to figure out what he was doing, and eventually he moved out of this stage.

During the grief and blame stages, some common mistakes can hinder recovery. Generalizing after any broken relationship is so easy to do. You take one isolated belief or experience and make it apply to life in general. How many times I've heard my counselees say, "All women are money-minded," "All men are losers," "All men are sex animals," "All women are full of emotions. They can't think." Such generalizations become immobilizers.

A frequent mistake is falling into the trap of living by a self-fulfilling prophecy. Perhaps you have heard it or said it: "I'll never find anyone else. I'm stuck in life. I'll always be single now." This faulty belief blinds us from seeing the possibilities around us. It gives us an attitude and look of defeat. Our self-fulfilling prophecy says more about where we are coming from than where we are going.

These prophecies do nothing but undermine and cripple relationships.

Another mistake we tend to carry over from a broken relationship is a set of unrealistic expectations. We use words like *should* and *must*, and when things don't happen according to our rigid set of beliefs, we perpetuate a life of disappointment. We use expectations for ourselves and for other people:

> "I have to be perfect for anyone to love me."

> "If I don't meet all his needs, he won't love me."

> "If she cares about me, she will . . . and she won't . . ."

> "If he reminds me of my former spouse or dating partner, he's not worth being with."

Wallowing in self-pity is an emotional trap that frequently follows a severed relationship. But indulging in self-pity blocks recovery and keeps other people from getting close.

One of the most destructive responses is not being able to look in the mirror. One day a man in my office made the statement, "Norm, I can't bear to face myself after what's happened in my life." Sometimes these people are best referred to as "runners." They are continually on the go and doing things to avoid having to deal with their situation and their feelings. They don't want to face themselves. The familiar patterns are incessant working, playing, being out each night, sleeping, watching TV, and worse yet, moving into alcohol and drugs. The frantic, hectic, busy life is just as bad as a withdrawn, lethargic existence.[33]

A very common mistake designed both to overcome the pain of the loss and to strike back is "revenge loving." The hurt person plunges into a new relationship prematurely out of anger. This revenge could manifest itself in three different styles.

One manifestation is to engage in a new relationship simply to make the other person jealous. A tremendous amount of energy is expended in this approach because arrangements are made so the ex-fiancée or spouse actually sees the new couple.

Another variation of revenge loving is acting out toward the new person in your life the way you were treated by your former partner. If abuse was part of the history and you were the victim, the tables are now turned. If manipulation was the pattern, in order not to be hurt again this becomes your weapon and defense.

A final variation of revenge loving is developing a relationship in which you are in control so no one can ever control and hurt you again. But in all three of these revenge styles, both you and the new person end up hurt, unhappy, and dissatisfied.[34]

There is a better way of draining anger. Revenge just doesn't work. Resentment punishes us more than the other person because most often the other individual isn't aware of the intensity of our feelings.

Magnification is also one of the traps and mistakes that occur after a broken relationship. You begin to think about the person you lost and are convinced he is having the time of his life while you are living in despair and discouragement. You feel limited and constrained, while you are sure your ex is living life to the fullest. The major phrase in your vocabulary is, "He is probably..." or "She is probably..."

Magnification can easily lead to martyrdom—if you let it. We all have a choice in how we respond.

Stage Four: Good-bye. This stage is often difficult to face, for it involves finality. If this stage is ignored or neglected, there won't be any recovery. This is when you really finally admit to yourself, "The relationship is over; this person is out of my life, and I have to go on." I have seen numerous people get stuck on the threshold of this stage, sometimes for more than a year. Some of them seem to move ahead, yet three weeks later they are asking the same questions and making the same statements about a reconciliation that will never happen. They are unwilling to say the final good-bye.

How do you say good-bye? Every relationship needs some type of eulogy. You need to face your feelings first.

Let's consider anger and resentment. Perhaps the initial step in overcoming anger and resentment is to take inventory and identify the hurt, anger, and resentment. One divorced man wrote:

> I am so angry at you for your lies and infidelities.
>
> I resent the fact that I have to pay you spousal support. It should be the other way around for what you did.
>
> I am wounded by your betrayal of me and our wedding vows.
>
> I am angry that you have the kids and they are being influenced by your lousy lifestyle and lack of morals.

Often, when a person begins listing these resentments, buried hurts and feelings begin climbing through the barriers. This list is for your own use and is not to be shared with anyone else except God. This is not an easy experience. You may find it very emotionally draining.

After you have made your list, go into a room and set up two chairs facing each other. Sit in one chair and imagine your ex sitting opposite you listening to what you are sharing. Put their name on a card or use a picture. Read your list out loud with your tone and inflections registering the feelings you have. Don't be concerned about editing what you are saying. Just get it out. Some people keep their list for days, adding to it as things come to mind. Others find it helpful to sit down and share like this several times for the drainage benefits. Don't be surprised to find yourself feeling angry, depressed, intense, embarrassed, or anxious. When you have concluded your time of sharing, spend a few minutes in prayer sharing these feelings with God and thanking Him for understanding what you are experiencing and for His presence in your life to help you overcome the feelings.

To become a free person and move forward in life, there is one additional step involved in the relinquishment of your anger and resentment. It is called forgiveness. No one can tell you when it will happen. You cannot hurry it up, for it is a process that takes time.

Most of us have our own set of reasons for not forgiving another person. We object to letting him or her off the hook, as it were. One of the ways to allow forgiveness to have a place in your life is to identify the objections you have to forgiving the person who hurt you so much. Take a blank sheet of paper and write a salutation at the top. Use the name of your former partner: "Dear _____." Underneath the salutation, write the words, "I forgive you for _____." Then complete the sentence by stating something your ex did that still hurts and angers you. Then capture the first thought that comes to mind after writing the sentence. It may be a feeling or thought that actually contradicts the forgiveness you are trying to express. It may be an emotional rebuttal or protest to what you have just written. Keep writing the "I forgive you for _____" statements for every thought or feeling that comes to the surface.

Your list may fill one page or even two. Don't be discouraged if your angry protests contradict the concept of forgiveness or are so firm and vehement that it seems as if you have not expressed any forgiveness at all. You are in the process of forgiving this person, so keep writing until all the pockets of resentment have been drained. Once again, show this list to no one, but using an empty chair, read the list aloud as though the person were sitting there listening to you.

Here is a sample of what a woman wrote to her former husband, who had divorced her:

Dear Jim,

I forgive you for not being willing to share your feelings with me.

"No, I don't. I still feel cheated by you. You were one way when we dated and then changed as soon as we were married."

I forgive you for withdrawing from me when I wanted to talk about our problems.

"I am still angry over your silence."

I forgive you for not trying to make our marriage work.

"Why couldn't you have tried more? We might have made it!"

I forgive you for sitting around watching TV when I wanted to go out and have fun.

"It's still hard for me to understand why you didn't want to be with me."

After she identified these as her main hurts, she continued to write these "forgiveness statements" each day for a week until she had no more rebuttals or complaints. When that happens, forgiveness is beginning.

Another way to do this is to take just one of the items you resent and write it again and again on the paper, listing every rebuttal that comes to mind until you can say, "I forgive you for _____" several times without any objection coming to mind. This will move you from living in the past to living in the present.

Perhaps Webster's definition of *forget* can give you some insight into the attitude and response you can choose. *Forget* means "to lose the remembrance of . . . to treat with inattention or disregard . . . to disregard intentionally; overlook; to cease remembering or noticing . . . to fail to become mindful at the proper time." It doesn't just happen. We do it intentionally, with purpose.

We are able to forgive because God has forgiven us. He has given us a beautiful model of forgiveness. Allowing God's forgiveness to permeate our lives and renew us is the first step toward wholeness.

In response to the question, "How do you know when you have forgiven a person?" Lewis Smedes once said, "You have forgiven when in your heart you begin to wish that person well." When we can pray for that person and ask for God's blessing upon him or her, we have forgiven. But again, it is gradual and may take months or years to work through the hurt and pain of the breakup.

To finalize your act of forgiveness, it may be helpful to write a statement of release to your ex. The woman described earlier, who was struggling to forgive her ex-husband, is a good example of what can happen in overcoming the hurt of the past. She said in her release statement:

Dear Jim,

I release you from the responsibility I gave you to determine how I have been feeling because of the divorce. I never did understand all that happened to make you the way you were, and I probably never will. It doesn't matter now. What matters is I release you from the bitterness and resentment I have held toward you over the past three years. I release you from my expectations of who and what you should have been. I forgive you.

Whether your previous relationship was a marriage or not, whether it ended by a divorce, death, or breaking up, a positive step is to write a good-bye letter. The following is an example of a letter a man wrote to his deceased wife when he was ready to remarry. Here is what he said:

A Good-Bye Letter

Dear Chrissie,

I want to get married again. I didn't want to wait and write you a "Dear-Chrissie-I-got-remarried" letter!

You know I loved you when you were here and we were together. Do I still love you? Yes and no. Yes, I still love the person I once knew, the one in my memory. But Chrissie, you aren't here anymore. I can't say "I love you," because there is no "you." I can cherish a thought, but I can't love it. Do I miss you? Yes. Do I wish I could see you again? Of course. But I am a person, and I can only love another person.

If you were here I would introduce you to Emily. She's attractive, kind and intelligent, and has a special kind of strength that I admire. She is also very affectionate to Aimee and Katie. She treats them kindly, very much as you did—although they do not see her as the authority figure you were!

I do miss you. And I miss our little Christine more than anyone—even you—could ever suspect. Please keep her warm. And please love her as only you can. I will love Katie and Aimee as only I now can.

Another step in this process is desensitizing painful places and locations. I have talked to people who have changed jobs, avoided restaurants and what used to be favorite recreational haunts, and even changed churches because they were painful reminders of what used to be. But this is allowing the other person to control and dominate your life. It is vital that you return to all these places and take control of them. Perhaps you vacationed at some special places before your divorce and you would like to return. But fear holds you back. Take a close friend or relative with you. Give this place to Jesus Christ in your prayers, and ask Him to take the pain away from that place. Go back to the restaurant or church. Make it a special time and ask God's blessing on the location and the occasion. The more you stay away, the greater your fear and aversion. By returning, you dilute the pain.

It is common to write a love letter in the building stage of a relationship. It is uncommon to write one to conclude a relationship, yet this practice can definitely put it to rest. This final love letter is one in which you collect all your thoughts, including anger, pleas, rationalizations, concerns, or apologies. Write it all in a letter, but do not mail it. This project could continue for several days, or it could be a one-time occurrence. It includes setting to rest your unfulfilled dreams with this person and what this individual will be missing out on because of not having you as a part of his or her life. This is a cleansing action, especially when you read the letter aloud to an empty chair, give all the contents to God in prayer, free yourself from the tyranny of these thoughts over you, and say your final good-bye. To complete the process, it helps to collect memories and even some actual items you were given by the person and reflect on the positive and negative memories. You may want to discard some and keep some.

Stage Five: Rebuilding and *Stage Six: Resolution.* At these stages, you are finally able to talk about the future with a sense of hope. You have just about completed your detachment from the other person, hopefully without lingering fears. Healthy new attachments may occur at this time without the past emotional attachment.

In meeting with a single parents' fellowship group, I asked a number of people to respond to the question, "What was the most helpful step you took to recover from a broken relationship?" Here are four different responses to show you the variety of methods.

> "Having a relationship with God, therefore, knowing I was not alone! My faith got me through! Having a place to go where I had people to relate to, and could get help, or express my feelings. Having a place (safe) (healthy) (Spirit-filled) where I was encouraged to grow and learn, where tools were given to make this possible."

> "I asked the person to be available to me whenever I had a question about why the relationship ended. He was able to answer questions I had and helped me understand what had happened in his mind. I call this "processing" what happened so I could *understand* it and then *accept* it. This was very freeing for me."

> "I have joined a support group which offers safe and positive relationships with Christians experiencing the same loss as I have. I have been able to reflect, learn, grow, cry, comfort and be comforted. I have experienced love and acceptance when I felt unlovable and unacceptable. I have begun to heal and begun to forgive."

"Taking stock in myself. I owned the problems that led to the break-up. I participated in group education targeted toward equipping people with tools and skills for recovery."

We need to remember, however, that there are three possible outcomes of a relationship breakup: a change for the better, a change for the worse, or a return to the previous level of living. At the outset of the breakup, it is almost impossible to conceive of things changing for the better, especially if you are the one who was rejected. In the latter stages of the crisis, you may be able to see glimmers of possibility for positive change. Your judgments and decisions during this turning point in your life will make the difference in the outcome. Then you can move forward.

"Why Aren't I Married Now, and What Can I Do About It?"

If you're single (and the chances are quite good that you are if you're reading this book), why are you? If you want to be married, why aren't you? What are the reasons? I don't mean the first obvious reasons that pop into your mind, but the real in-depth reasons that are at the core of your situation in life at the present time.

Reasons for Being Single

I'll admit I'm a list-maker. Part of the reason is we think and evaluate better when we can see our reasons rather than just think them. You may be surprised by what you write, especially if you take several days for this process. Take some time and reflect on your own reasons before you consider some of the ones I've heard over the years:

1. I just haven't found Mr. or Mrs. Right yet.

2. I enjoy being alone.

3. I don't have sufficient time to give to a relationship. When would I do it?

4. Some of those "unique characteristics" of the opposite sex I could live without.

5. I haven't met the person that meets the criteria on my list.

6. I believe it's OK to be single (I think).

7. I've been single 40 years. I don't know if I can or want to adjust. Maybe the other person won't either.

8. I'm still undergoing damage reconstruction from my last relationship.

9. I just don't like the dating scene. Most places are a meat market.

10. I'm not sure if I'm ready yet. I need to be prepared.

11. I like my independence, and I see marriage as restrictive.

12. What if I pick a loser? I'm good at that.

13. As a woman, I am afraid of being dominated by a man. I could lose my identity.

14. I've been divorced twice now. I'm gun-shy.

15. What if I love them, but they end up not loving me?

16. I'm gun-shy over this intimacy stuff. It may not be for me.

17. Where do you go to find a Christian partner?

18. I can't juggle work and dating.

19. Can you fit a vocation and a wife together?

20. Is there anyone who's a Christian that's really sharp?

21. Where do you go to meet a winner? I know where the losers are....

22. There are no strong men out there. If I have to nurture or mother them, they're not worth all the trouble. I haven't found many yet who have any domestic competence and those that do are perfectionistic, inflexible, and I would be miserable trying to live with them.

23. Most women I've met are too pushy. Yeah, they seem to accept me at first, but they have a reform school mentality and can't wait to begin "improving" me.

Realities for Those Wanting to Marry

If you do want to be married, there are several conditions that will have to be met. They are as follows:

1. You will have to take risks. (But that's how you move ahead in life. Remember the turtle. It only makes progress when it sticks its neck out.)

2. You will experience hurt. (But you've experienced that before and survived, haven't you?)

3. You cannot duplicate your single lifestyle in a marriage relationship. (You may like what you have now, but marriage and all its benefits can be better. If you think I'm an advocate of marriage, you're right. In premarital counseling I share with the couple, "You cannot bring your

single lifestyle into marriage. Let's identify now the changes that you will need to make." Each change carries with it the potential for growth.)

4. Your career may not have the same amount of energy, time, and attention given to it as you give now. (Is that so bad? There's more to life than work, and if you're building your identity and self-esteem through your work, this is an opportunity to change.)

5. You will need to become vulnerable and intimate. (There's nothing negative about that. It will help you fulfill the potential that God has given to you to be fully human.)

If you value being single more than these, then reconsider marriage. Otherwise, failure to meet the above criteria could destroy a marriage. The major question may be, "What is there in your life, good or bad, that is competing with your desire to be married?" Is there something that is more important than being married? What could be a higher priority? As one man in his forties shared with me, "Yes, I want to be married, but I've got to get this new job off the ground first. I just can't do both at the same time and do justice to both. I need to eat and pay my bills, so I guess you know which one is going to have to wait."

Having reasons for not getting married isn't a negative. Not everyone is called to be married. Have you ever given any thought to a chosen single lifestyle?

The Value of Singleness

Consider what Tim Stafford has said about singleness:

God may want you to be single. He wants everyone to be single for at least a part of life. And the

Bible doesn't talk about singleness as second-rate. In fact, it speaks of it positively. In the Middle Ages Christians went too far, and *marriage* was regarded as second-rate. We seem to have swung the other way now, and need to balance in the middle. Both marriage and singleness are gifts from God.

Ponder for a minute one fact: Jesus Christ, our Lord, never married. He never had sexual intercourse. Yet He was perfect, and perfectly fulfilled. He lived the kind of life we want to imitate. That doesn't mean we ought to all want to be single: there's no doubt marriage is the best way for most men and women. But it should say one thing for certain: singleness need not be unhappy.

Paul wasn't married either, at least at the height of his career. He wrote recommending the single life in 1 Corinthians 7, calling it a gift. (Strange that this is the one gift most would prefer to exchange.) And Jesus Himself, in Matthew 19:10-12, talks positively about the reasons some people should remain unmarried. . . .

One of the saddest things I see, then, is the tendency for single people to live life as though waiting for something or someone to happen to them. They act as though they are in limbo, waiting to become capable of life when the magic day at the altar comes. Of course, they're usually disappointed. In some cases they become such poor specimens of humanity that no one wants to marry them. More often they do get married only to discover that they haven't received the key to life: the initiative and character they should have developed before marriage is exactly what they need in marriage. And they are still lonely and frustrated. . . .

Our culture, especially our Christian culture, has stressed repeatedly that a good marriage takes work. It holds up for admiration those who have formed "a good marriage." But I've seldom heard anyone emphasize the fact that a good single life also takes work. I've never heard anyone compliment a person for having created a good single lifestyle. This creates an atmosphere in which telling single people they have received a gift is rather like convincing a small child that liver ought to taste good, because it's "good for you."

Singleness, as I see it, is not so much a state we've arrived at as an open door, a set of opportunities for us to follow up.[35]

Charles Cerling suggests the following thoughts to determine if singleness is for you:

1. Recognize that singleness may be for a period of time (for example, until you are 30), rather than for all of your life.

2. Recognize that it is easier to decide that singleness is not for you and get married than to realize you should have remained single once you are married.

3. Are you able to live with the idea that you might remain single all your life?

4. Is your desire to serve God complicated by the thought of a marriage partner?

5. Are you able to enjoy yourself without feeling the need for a lot of dates?

6. Could you live out the conditions of a vow to God to remain single for a period of time (for example, one year, five years, etc.) without seriously dating?

7. Do you see the advantages of singleness out-weighing the advantages of marriage?

8. Do you see God calling you to a form of service that would be difficult if you were married (for example, work in the inner city, work in primitive mission projects)?

9. Are you willing to live with the stigma of being single if this is what God wants?

10. If you think singleness is for you, try it for a specific period of time. (Go for one year without a date, devoting your normal dating time to serving God.) If you fail, there should be no thought of having fallen out of favor with God. This is just an experiment. It is similar to trying to go to the mission field and finding that you can't. You can still serve God effectively wherever you are. However, you should be as open to God's call to single living as you are to any other call He might give you.[36]

What do you think about his suggestions?

One thoughtful woman shared her experience with me in a letter.

My dating experience has been vast indeed considering the fact that I am now 41 years old and still unmarried. Not only is the experience deep, I would say it is also very broad—the sheer variety in men I have either dated or ended up having more serious relationships with is quite staggering when I think back on the various personalities.

Still after all that, I have not yet been motivated by any particular relationship to commit myself to a man for my lifetime. Possibly that has been a matter of where I was in my own personal growth or possibly it was a matter of not having yet met the man I will marry. Being such a romantic it will be a hard reality to look back and find that marriage was not in the plan for me, but I have never quite been able to accept that thought as coming from the Lord so I am still hoping to find the man of my dreams. . . .

It is important to come to grips with the reality that marriage may not happen. I guess I say that because I've watched so many of my friends pine away for a man and put their life on hold until they were married, only to still not be married or eventually marry into a relationship that was less than fulfilling. Having observed that phenomenon for many years, I decided to *live* my life no matter who was or was not in it: friends, family, dating relationships, career, etc. There is so much in life to experience that I would hate to miss all that life offers waiting for someone to share it with. Better I think to live it as best you can hoping always for a companion, but learning to deal with all the feelings and realities that are present when you are by yourself. Besides I think men and women who have truly resolved some of the issues of being alone and creating a life that can stand apart from an intense connection with another person, may make the happiest and healthiest marriage partners anyway.

Singleness is only a problem when you want to be married, but you resist it and don't know why. You end up being stuck. If you were to get married in the next year, what changes would occur in your life? Make a list of the benefits and then make a list of the negatives.

The Case For and Against Marriage

<u>Positive</u>   <u>Negative</u>

Now go back over your list once again. How could you reframe each negative so it might become a positive? Think about it. Many singles that I talk to want to marry. There is no question of that. The issue is how to go about finding the right person. That's what we need to consider next.

Is the Laundromat the only place to meet people? One of the teachers who influenced me the most as a therapist was a psychiatrist by the name of William Glasser. A concept that he drilled into us was, "You've got to have a plan for what you want to get out of life." Plan-making is easier for some than for others, however. Some people reading this book will have a personality bent that sees a plan as an unnecessary piece of luggage. It gets in the way of their free-spirited endeavors. But having a master plan for where and how to meet other singles is important.

Even with a plan in mind, timing is a big part of discovering the right person. Meeting the right person and getting married is tied into timing more than you realize. Perhaps you've experienced this already. One evening you may have met the type of person you'd been seeking for years. But wouldn't you know it! You either meet them at a function where you're on your first date with a possessive person you could care less about, and they scare the other "possibility" away. Or you're three months into a relationship and just beginning to develop some closeness. Or perhaps this special person is already dating or engaged to your best friend. These situations will happen.

Four Relationship Possibilities

Your relationships are probably going to be one of four possibilities: the right person at the wrong time; the wrong person at the right time; the wrong person at the wrong time; or finally (and hopefully), the right person at the right time.[37]

The right person but the wrong time leaves you thinking, "If only I could have met them at another time." Perhaps you met such a person when you were too young, too broke, or too afraid. You end up with a lot of "what ifs," and this illusive person stays at the forefront of your mind for months.

The wrong person at the right time can lead to some disastrous results. This can be very painful for you if you have high romantic hopes and they have none. You may try even harder at this time to make a relationship work. Sometimes you begin wondering what is wrong with you! The real problem occurs because the desire to settle down and get married is so strong that you tend to be less objective in your evaluation of the other person. The desire to be married takes precedence over properly evaluating the person. The statement: "I just want to be married" is said with such intensity and force that it's apparent the screening apparatus has been put in neutral.

I've heard many women say, "I'm not getting any younger. The window of opportunity for having children is slowly closing, and I need to get married in the next two years and have a baby right away if I don't want to miss out. I need a marriage-prone man right away." This need can become so intense that you may decide to fall in love with the next romantic interest that comes along. Several men and women that I saw when they were in the midst of a divorce made virtually the same statement: "Whatever possessed me to marry that person? He/she wasn't really the person for whom I was looking. My head must have been in the clouds. I guess I just wanted to be married so bad I took the first available one."

For many singles, their life seems to be a continuous pattern of the wrong person at the wrong time. It's especially difficult when there's a strong attraction to the person, but you know that's not the person for you. Fortunately, most of these relationships are short-lived unless one person hangs on because "any relationship is better than none." Sometimes, though, I've seen relationships last for years where one or both persons keep trying to make it fit together or feel, "Perhaps someday I will really love them." Sometimes relationships develop into lasting platonic friendships which at least fill that need for the couple.

Naturally, you want the right person at the right time. And this is possible.

Self-Evaluation

Before we plunge into the plans and procedures for finding that right person, there's another factor to consider. Let's say you meet a prospective partner—what do you have to offer that will attract that person to you? What are your qualities, your attributes, your pluses, your minuses? Sometimes we are caught up more in *finding* the right person than in *becoming* the right one. Perhaps it would be beneficial to write a paragraph describing your marriage relationship value (MRV). That may give you a better basis for making your selection. You may be wondering, What do I say about myself? Describe who you are, especially indicating your qualities, interests, personality characteristics, including both positive and negative.

Putting it another way, when you place your order for the type of person you want, is your order likely to be filled? What I mean is, are you personally the type of person who will draw the kind of person you want? If you're negative and critical, what are the odds that you will attract a positive, healthy person? If you're positive and secure, you're more likely to attract someone like that. So . . . cultivate in yourself what you want in a partner.

Perhaps these statements I've collected from what some singles were looking for will help you add additional significant facts.

"I want someone who is economically sound, who doesn't have a bunch of outstanding bills, and makes $75,000-$100,000 per year." Here it sounds like economic stability is important, but what do you have to offer this person economically? Is your desire for this based upon your standard of living, or do you need someone like this to bail you out of a life of indebtedness? Would the other person be secure with your economic status?

"I want someone who is out of school and climbing the vocational ladder. I'd like their job to have significance in society and make a contribution to the lives of others." My question would be, What is there in your life that draws such a person to you? Did you hope to live vicariously through this person and their attainments, or can you match what you're asking for in this relationship? Will the relationship be equal or one-sided?

"I want a woman who is really attractive. It's not everything, but I need to have someone at whom I enjoy looking. She doesn't have to be a '10,' but a '9 ½' would help." It is important that we enjoy the sight of the other person, but will this person enjoy looking at you just as much? Are you able to give what you expect your partner to contribute?

And before you return to your task of writing the paragraph about yourself, there is one other factor to consider. You will be looking for and drawn to a person who has certain characteristics and qualities. Let's say that you marry a person who is either economically stable, has a highly contributing occupation, or is highly attractive. What will happen to your marriage commitment if five years after the wedding your spouse loses his/her job and is unemployable for two years? Or if he no longer has a vocation filled with status or that contributes to society? Or what if she gains 80 pounds or experiences disfiguring burns over 40 percent of the body? It has happened. You never believe it will happen to you—only to someone else. It's something to think about.

You may be thinking this personal paragraph is a chore. Do people really do this? Yes, they do all the time, either for themselves or whenever they become involved in some sort of a singles' dating referral service. Here are some examples taken from a Christian dating periodical in California:

TOM SELLECK LOOK ALIKE
Handsome, 6'1/2", 195 lbs., 40, never married. Enjoys sports, theater. Home owner. Emotionally available. Good communicator. Seeking positive, relaxed disposition woman with good heart, emotionally available, unencumbered, kind and humorous. Prefer never married, 5'-5'7", 23-33. In good shape physically, emotionally, financially.

ROMANTIC, SUCCESSFUL, HANDSOME
Degreed professional, 6', 180 lbs., 40s, muscular, fit, DWM, sensitive, playful. Likes Bible studies, concerts, walks, your kids, learning. Seeking happy, bright, kind, supportive, attractive, slender, fit, secure, affectionate, confident, 30s/40s, S/DWF, full photo, please.

COME FIND ME!
SWF, 34, affectionate, educated, fun and friendly, (cute with curves!), career-minded and self-reliant. Enjoys dancing, music, active sports, family, singing/church, and entertaining/home. Seeking dynamic, self-assured and polished gentleman to love. My man: bright, ambitious, playful, spontaneous, likes laughter, enjoys people, wants marriage and family. No smokers, no drugs.

STATUESQUE, ATTRACTIVE, WARM
Degreed SDA lady, 58, 5'9". Seeks committed Christian friend to enjoy theater, symphony, travel, boats, swimming, walks, dining. Please be tall, solvent, educated, sensitive, caring, health conscious, non-smoking, no drugs, with high, spiritual goals.

Keep in mind these ads were placed in a Christian Datemate Connection newspaper and each person is hoping for responses. I'm quite sure they were written for that purpose. To help in the objectivity process in creating your own paragraph, there are two steps you could take. One would be to interview several close friends and relatives who know you very well and ask them the following questions:

1. What are some adjectives you would use to describe me, both positive and negative?
2. What are some of my strengths?
3. What are some of my weaknesses?
4. What do you think I have to offer a marriage partner?
5. What do you think I need more of to make a marriage work?
6. Describe the qualities and personality characteristics of the person you think would be best for me.

"That's difficult!" you may protest. I agree. These are hard questions. Many readers will say, "Forget it" and keep on reading. To hear the perspective of others may arouse hurt and defensiveness. Yet if you do ask other people, realize that you've asked for their opinion. Keep in mind it is their perspective. It's not fact. Prior to asking them, however, read the following verses. They may help. "If you refuse criticism you will end in poverty and disgrace; if you accept criticism you are on the road to fame" (Proverbs 13:18 TLB). "It is a badge of honor to accept valued criticism" (Proverbs 25:12 TLB). "A man who refuses to admit his mistakes can never be successful. But if he confesses and forsakes them, he gets another chance" (Proverbs 28:13 TLB).

The other (and less threatening) possibility is to write your descriptive paragraph and ask these same people to read it. They could either comment upon it, add to it, or suggest deletions. Either choice you make could give you significant information.

It's not only important to consider whom you may end up with, but put yourself in their place and consider with whom they will end up. There are two difficult questions, but they've got to be answered. Be sure to complete all ten responses for each question.

Why would someone want to be married to me?

1.   6.
2.   7.
3.   8.
4.   9.
5.   10.

Why might a person not want to be married to me?

1.   6.
2.   7.
3.   8.
4.   9.
5.   10.

Your "Perfect Partner"

Let's consider that "perfect partner" you're looking for by considering some basic practical questions. Hopefully this process will lead you to a better understanding of what you want and what you don't want in a marriage partner.

Some information you may want to know about a prospective partner could include the following:

—Vocational information

—Current job

—Past jobs

—Education and training—additional education needed or desired.

—How well do they do in their job? Promotions? Reason for termination of past jobs. How do they feel about their present job? Amount of time spent in their job. Do they expect to continue in this occupation?

—Who else do they support? Amount of debts. Do they balance their checkbook regularly?

— Have they ever made more than they do now? Do they have an investment program?

—Friendships—many or few? Do they prefer to socialize or hang around home?

Let me suggest other topic areas which need to be explored. You may want to write out some of your own questions to ask.

—Their Christian experience

—Interests and hobbies

—Drugs, smoking and alcohol habits, current and past

—Family relationships and involvement

—Emotional life and personality characteristics

Could you answer these or not? Have you ever considered these factors?

Sometimes people are overbalanced on one side or the other. They either know what they don't want, but don't know what they do want, or they know what they want, but are unsure of what they don't want. You need both.

I like to suggest a checklist which involves three categories: Optional, Would Like to Have, and Must Have. Here is a partial list for you to consider; you can add to it. And keep in mind that it's better to do this evaluation before searching than after marriage.

	Optional	Would Like	Must Have
College education			
Christian			
Loves outdoors			
Enjoys theater			
Good dancer			
Never married			
No children			
Trustworthy			
Outgoing			
Quiet/reserved			
Prayerful			
Sports fan			
Flexible			
Thoughtful			
Sense of humor			
Affectionate			
Wants kids			
Nondrinker			
Willing to travel			
Enjoys hunting			
Good listener			
Detailed communicator			
Similar in age			
Extrovert			
Likes dogs			
Likes cats			
Steady employment			
Debt-free			

Now add to the list those items which are high priorities to you and evaluate them. Then answer the question, "What do you want this person to be like 10 years from now, 20 years, 30 years?"

Some people believe they can love someone before they know the person. The only thing you love with this belief is a fantasy. Lasting love is based on knowledge of a person and not on assumptions and dreams. It takes time and hundreds of hours of in-depth, revealing discussion.

Conventional dating patterns actually waste time and prolong the process of getting to know one another. When you spend time together (if your purpose is to find a spouse), avoid time spent watching TV, movies, and plays. Interact with each other rather than be passively entertained.

Initial Contacts—A Screening Process

One author suggests that the initial contacts be used as a screening process. There are three phases to the screening.

1. Your first step is to determine if there is something special about the person. Are they worth more than a ten-minute conversation? If you're unsure, is it worth investing more time to see if your initial impression is accurate? If not, don't waste your time.

2. Are the person's values and goals compatible with yours? Imagine how their values and goals would affect you over the next ten years. Could you live with them for the rest of your life? If not, why waste your time!

3. Marriage is social. Your spouse doesn't just relate to you, but to others. Does the way this

person relates to others meet your standards or expectations? Are you embarrassed by what they do? Do you have to explain away their behavior or excuse it to others? If so, do you want a lifetime of this?[38]

Some might say, "Where does God and the leading of His Spirit fit into this? Isn't this taking the choice out of His hands? What about His will for my life?" Have you ever considered that taking these steps could enable you to better discover His will? That's a good possibility.

You may find other people saying to you, "Be realistic. If you're going to find someone to marry, you'd better adjust those standards. The man or woman you want exists in only one spot—*your mind*!" It's true you have to be realistic, but our society is filled with those who didn't marry the person they wanted; they simply settled. The problem is more in not clarifying what you want in advance, searching, finding, building a solid relationship, and experiencing the rigors of premarital counseling.

Once you identify those items you must have, don't allow yourself to waiver or think, "It's not that important." Just remember it was and probably still is important. One man in his thirties shared an interesting insight:

Norm, I had my list of what I wanted, but then one day I met this woman who didn't have any of the six qualities that I said were 'Must Haves.' I fell for her. The attraction was intense. We started going together and it was great. I wondered why I didn't miss those qualities.

Six months later, the attraction was subsiding and there wasn't much left. It was then that I saw how those qualities would have kept us together. I also realized it was also a case of meeting the wrong person at the right time.

I dated around for two years and one day Jean and I met. You'll never guess where—in the checkout line when I ran over her foot with my grocery cart! It was worth the wait.

Be patient. Wait.
This is what one man shared with me:

It seems like I have been waiting all my life for God to bring the right person into my life for marriage. I had waited until the age of 33 and thought that the Lord had brought that right person into my life for marriage. We had dated for almost a year and had become what I had thought the best of friends. But as I look back now, I can see that I was very shallow in my observations and questions that I had in dating in general. I thought if the other person said that they were a born again Christian, then that was what they meant. I really didn't think I'd have to look or dig any deeper or question what their beliefs really were.

As we dated, I continued to run through red flags. I didn't relate to them as being red flags, though, until I looked back after the divorce and wondered how I could have missed many of them. I also realized some of them were so hidden within her that they didn't come to the surface until after the divorce.

It has now been over seven years since the divorce. As I look back and see how my ideals and expectations have changed, I am so grateful to the Lord that I didn't meet anyone or fall in love in the first several years. I can see that even though I felt that I was ready, I wasn't even close to being ready for remarriage.

I must admit, it has been lonely at times and it would be wonderful to have that special person to share things with, but I am glad that I have not married or settled for less than what I really am wanting and looking for.

I have had friends tell me to just pray and the Lord will provide, but I don't think that it is always that easy. I totally believe in the power of prayer, and sometimes people do meet their spouses in the grocery store or in Sunday School. But if you are not finding her there, yes, you need to pray, but you must get out and leave no stones unturned if a mate is what you are really looking for. It is kind of like looking for the Lord's direction in finding a job. You don't say a prayer and just sit by the phone and wait for it to ring. You have to go out and knock on doors and genuinely seek employment. At the same time you have to know what type of work that you are looking for. And in searching for the right mate you have to know ahead of time, to a degree, what you are looking for, your expectations and what your negotiables and nonnegotiables are in a mate and in a relationship.

For me, in leaving no stones unturned I have attended church singles' groups, Christian singles' dances, networked with friends with some of their friends, had a nice Christian yenta lady looking for me, and have tried Christian singles' connection ads. I have found that all of these things have merit, and I have met a number of wonderful ladies. However, I have also met a number of strange ladies, so one must use discernment and not be embarrassed in asking questions.

I've seen numerous couples who have experienced the "three-to-six month syndrome." They had an instant attraction to one another and it was intense—almost overwhelming. They just clicked. Sometimes they say, "It was as though I knew this person all of my life . . . and we just met!" The relationship builds rapidly, and they're in love. The topic of marriage is hinted at occasionally, and it flits in and out of their conversation from time to time. But the longer they go together . . . something happens. Perhaps one isn't as eager as the other or one withdraws a bit or one doesn't pursue with the same fervor. The romantic high seems to be a bit tarnished. They begin to struggle with some issues that have emerged, and now they have to work at the relationship for the first time. Instead of being totally impressed with their partner, they are scrutinizing and appraising them. My response to this is "Wonderful!" This is great! This is positive. Now you have the opportunity to see the other person for who they really are. Now the relationship has an opportunity to grow.

It is possible to have standards that are too high. And sharing your list or vision of who you want to marry with trusted friends may help bring your expectations in line.

The Social Exchange Theory

Let's consider your list in a new way, since the person you have described as the person you want to marry has a message for you. Is this person your equal or the opposite? Are you attracted to those who are as financially secure, educated, or as attractive as you? Are they on your level? Or do you tend to date "up" or "down"? It doesn't mean you are identical, but there will be some trade-offs. A relationship tends to sustain itself when each person feels they are receiving something from the other person and perhaps more than they would receive in another relationship. If you are not getting that much from a relationship, you may leave it even if no one else is available.

You've probably heard the phrase "He's a good catch" or "She's a good catch." One of my close friends and fishing enthusiasts has his own variation on this phrase. He says as he begins a new relationship (using fishing lingo), "She's a keeper." This is what most people are looking for. The people you are most likely to date are those who have romantic desirability levels equal to yours.

I don't want to become theoretical on you, but I've been talking about the social-exchange theory. This theory states that even falling in love is not a happenstance event, but more of a deliberate process. The theory is that before you allow yourself to become involved with another person, you consciously or unconsciously try to discern if that person is your romantic equal. The majority of men and women use their perception of their own level of romantic desirability to determine the suitability of that other person.

But there's more. Reflect back on your past several relationships. Were the individuals distinctively different in their physical characteristics? Was there a wide variation in the way they looked, or were there more similarities than dissimilarities? Have you been attracted to those who tend to look alike or dissimilar? Many people after reflecting back have discovered a common theme of similar physical characteristics in their partners. Many have a picture in their mind of what their spouse-to-be should look like. Perhaps you do and it has been operating like radar scanning out prospective partners. If you have done this in the past and are just now becoming aware of it, is this what you really want? Are looks so high on your criteria list that this limits you from finding those people with other characteristics that are more important to you? That's why it is so vital for you to write the descriptive paragraph about yourself.

I know that some of you who are reading this will say, "That's too scientific, too calculating, too logical. It just doesn't work like that!" Most people do not fall in love by chance or at random. There's more to it than meets the eye; it's just not obvious. Many of the items on the "Must Have" list are the variables which will affect mate selection. It may sound unromantic, but there's a lot more involved in romance and finding that right person than we realize.[39]

Who have you dated in the past? What were they like? How do they match up to who you are looking for now? List the names of the last five people with whom you had a relationship, and then describe each person based on what we have covered so far in this chapter.

Name: _____

  Similarities?

  Dissimilarities?

  "Must Haves" That They Had

Now, think back about some of your most pleasant relationships. Was the person more similar to you or dissimilar? Think about it. Even though you have your list of qualities, and you like certain physical characteristics, the most pleasant and productive romantic relationships tend to be with those who have similar *beliefs*, *attitudes*, and especially *values*. When you date someone and think you have found these three, be sure you investigate to see how long they've held them. These qualities may have been a quick recent acquisition in order to impress you, but there are no roots.

How have you reacted to people that you've met socially or at work who don't have the same beliefs, attitudes, and values, and are not a romantic possibility? Did you want to be around them? Did you want to invest time with them? Were you that comfortable with them? Most of us aren't and, if that's the case, why would anyone think they could spend the rest of their life with a person like that? Incompatibility in the area of beliefs, attitudes, and values is often fatal in a marriage. If you are in constant disagreement with your partner, that's not very enjoyable. If your partner shares your beliefs and values, it draws you closer, rather than repelling you.

When a person finally marries, does he choose a person just the opposite of himself? For years the statement "opposites attract" has been used to explain part of the attraction process. And yet the results of hundreds of studies of married couples indicate that, almost without exception, in physical, social, and psychological characteristics the mates are more alike than different. The exceptions, or those that appear to be exceptions, do not alter this overall tendency.

Complementary and Contradictory Characteristics

Within the framework of like marrying like, however, some characteristics appear to be quite opposite in each spouse. Since the fulfillment of needs is at the heart of such mate selection, one will find that some needs in couples are complementary whereas some are contradictory.

It is in the area of complementary characteristics and needs that the concept "opposites attract" is seen to be somewhat accurate. The most important complementary needs involve dominance and submissiveness. If a person has a need to dominate, he will tend to marry and be gratified by a person who needs to be submissive. If a man marries a woman who has the need to be dominant and he is submissive, there may be some conflict if the social expectations of society call for the male to be dominant and the female to be submissive. In spite of social pressures, many couples may choose to go against the expectation. If one has a need to nurture others, such as giving sympathy, love, protection, and indulgence, he would be happy with a partner who has the need to be nurtured. (Most people, fortunately, are capable of both. That's healthier.) A person who needs to admire and praise others would enjoy being married to a person who needs to receive respect and admiration. If the needs of one spouse change years later, the relationship could be disrupted. Complementary needs help determine how two people treat each other.

It is important to keep in mind the distinction between complement and contradiction. Unfortunately, some couples label any difference between themselves as complementary. Complementary needs fit so well together that no compromise is required. However, contradictory needs require a compromise on some middle ground, but not usually on a happy medium. For example, if one is extremely thrifty and the other is a big spender, the needs will clash head-on. If one enjoys social contacts and the other is a recluse, conflict is almost inevitable.

In our American culture, people choose a partner whom they expect to be gratifying to them. It is interesting to note that both engaged and married couples see things in each other that cannot be found through testing. What an individual sees in another person is what pleases him. "What would ever attract him to that girl?" we ask, because we cannot see in her the things he sees. A couple's choice of each other is based upon a set of relationships pleasing to themselves, which they attribute to one another. Have you ever experienced this in your relationships?

As people date and are attracted to one another, basic needs are met. Much of a couple's relationship is based upon the meeting of those needs. This means that there are literally thousands of people of the opposite sex who could fulfill those needs if the person has appropriate status qualities. Being held in esteem in someone else's eye confirms our worth in our own eyes. The need to fall in love and to have someone else fall in love with us does not require a particular person. The first step is having those basic needs met. Then the details of "personality meshing" can be filled in imaginatively. This personality meshing probably determines the future of the relationship established by a couple.

Couples who marry for healthy reasons and those who marry for unhealthy reasons have basically the same motivating forces propelling them toward marriage, but their intensity varies.

Most individuals are attracted to one another by dependency needs. We all have these needs, no matter how healthy we are. Healthy dependency needs reflect a desire to experience completion. With unhealthy dependency needs, there is a desire for completion *and* for possession.

Self-esteem and its potential for enhancement propel people toward marriage. Everyone wants to receive affirmation of worth and value from another person. Some have the excessive need for their spouses to make them feel worthy, good, attractive, wanted, desired, and so on. Gradually the excessive need can exact a strain upon the relationship.

The normal desire for affirmation, however, is also a strong attracting and maintaining force of marriage. The desire of increased self-esteem and dependency needs both build commitment, which has been called the glue of marriage. That glue is in the process of setting when a couple arrives for premarital instruction.

Two therapists who have specialized in premarital preparation pass along this insight:

> Our assumption that marriage is neither accidental nor dichotomous has been influenced by our clinical practice with the hundreds of couples we have seen both in marital counseling and in premarital counseling. In thinking about these couples and the manner in which they chose each other, we have discovered that the couples were apparently performing a task and involved in a process. It has struck us that many couples were involved in the task of finding some way to initiate growth. The growth could be in many areas. Perhaps it was in becoming more outgoing, more self-confident, more intimate, or some other dimension of their personality that they felt needed expansion. The mate they chose, therefore, from the millions of individuals available was exactly the person who could provide them with the kind of growth they needed. Some women, for example, seek out a particular man who can teach them to be tough, just as some men seek out a woman who can teach them to be soft. It almost seems to us that couples in some way find each other and choose each other on the basis of their potential to induce change. It is as if couples are in a strange way performing the task of therapy. Perhaps we could say that marriage is an amateur attempt at psychotherapy.
>
> All of this is a way of saying that we believe that marriage is purposeful and that couples choose each other on the basis of the ability of the other person to help them initiate growth. We think that couples are involved in a task of healing. It is as if

many individuals at the point of dating and moving to marriage find themselves to be incomplete in some way. Their search for a mate is not haphazard, but rather based on some kind of deeply intuitive homing device that relentlessly and purposely pursues exactly the kind of person who will provide them with the stimulation for the growth they are seeking.[40]

Cultural Definitions of the Ideal Mate

Further complicating the selection of your partner is the factor of the cultural "ideal mate" image, depending upon what marriage means in a particular society. This is loosening up somewhat, but it still exists. If, for example, marriage is primarily a division of labor and child-rearing, the ideal wife would be one who is physically strong with broad shoulders and broad hips. Descriptions of masculine and feminine characteristics provided by a culture influence the ideal mate images. In one society the ideal woman is sweet and delicate, in another she is extroverted and sexually provocative. Culture defines it; we fit into the pattern. What does your church expect of you in choosing a life partner? Your friends? Your parents? I've had parents call me to tell me the person their son or daughter is marrying doesn't fit their ideal!

Cultural definitions of the ideal mate can influence mate selection in two ways. Because this definition identifies what is desirable in a mate, it almost labels the desirability of each person. The closer a person gets to this cultural ideal, the more attractive he or she becomes to a greater number of people. And if the person realizes that he is approaching the ideal, he can be more selective in his own choice of a mate and hold out for the one closest to the ideal.

The second way in which this cultural definition of the ideal mate can influence mate selection is called "idealization of the mate." It means that, even if your choice does not meet the cultural standard of idealization, you attribute those characteristics to the person with whom you have fallen in love. You rationalize because you're fighting against the standard.

The choice of the partner is complicated by this human penchant for wishful thinking. Unfortunately, the more insecure a person is, the greater is his need for idealizing his partner. That's alarming since the idealization vanishes in the first year.

Most people do not think about mate selection in a logical, analytical manner, but we are unconsciously influenced by these factors and in subtle ways we probably do adhere to them. Yet many people would vehemently deny these ideas, protesting that "It is our love that brought us together." Yes, love plus these factors are present.

If cultural images influence one's selection of a mate, what about images that your parents have of your future mate? Parents exert considerable indirect control over the associations of their children; this in turn limits the field of possibilities for mate selection. College students feel this pressure less than those who remain at home. Parents help determine an acceptable grouping of eligibles from which their child may choose a mate. Interestingly, one study shows that when a woman's parents disapproved of her relationship with a young man, more than twice as many relationships ended in broken engagements or early divorce as when both parents approved. The approval of the man's parents does not seem to be nearly as important.[41]

When you reflect on the kind of person that you are looking for, consider these three questions:

1. Are these your criteria or your parents'? To what extent are their wishes coming out in the person for whom you're looking? And if you discover their influence, why do they want you with this person? Perhaps you need to review what their desires are.

2. Are your criteria leftovers from an earlier stage in your life? Your needs, desires, and priorities for a partner will be different at age 20, 30, 40, and 50. Be sure to rethink what you're looking for now and why.

3. Are your friends' or church's expectations a major part of your mate selection? They may be subtle in their suggestions, but they may be there just the same. If you're gifted musically, you may experience pressure to marry someone who is also musical or going into the ministry or who will remain in the area so your abilities won't be lost. It has happened!

Let's ask yet another question. Where did you meet your former prospects? Did you just "bump" into one another, or were you at an event where it was likely you might meet someone? Did you realize that most often mate selection has some very unromantic facets to it? For example, physical location is a very significant limitation for a relationship. The farther two people live apart, the more likely they are to choose someone who lives closer. Driving an hour or two each way while maintaining a full-time job, church involvement, social events, and family commitments leads to diminishing returns. Often those who meet at a camp, convention, or seminar and begin a relationship find it very difficult to maintain it from a distance with the amount of time and energy needed. There is a limit to how much time and money a person will spend traveling to see someone when others are nearby.

You've been given a lot to consider in this chapter. This is just the beginning. Many of you are saying, "Where do I find the person? Where do I look?" That's next.

"Where Do I Meet Them and What Do I Say?"

was in the supermarket three blocks from my house. Every Thursday night I was there getting the groceries I need. I came to the end of an aisle and looked right but turned left... and I saw her. She was sharp, not stunning, but sharp. As I cruised by (I have this great peripheral vision) I glanced at her left hand and, *hallelujah*, no wedding ring. She was someone I wanted to meet. She didn't have any kids with her, so that was another plus for me. I kept about twenty yards behind her, and even though I'd selected everything on my list, I kept looking as though I was looking for more items. I was planning my time so I could get in the checkout line right behind her and strike up a conversation.

She headed for the checkout line and so did I. A family with five noisy kids was headed the same direction and I could see that they might cut me off and beat me there. I gunned the shopping cart and cut a corner real close. Too close, in fact. My foot hit the display of two hundred tightly stacked cans of beans. They began to tumble slowly at first and then an avalanche. As they did their thing, I did mine. I fell. Flat on my face! And as I did, I involuntarily shoved the shopping cart and it took off. You guessed it! It shot across the floor on a straight line towards that attractive woman. It was a perfect shot. Right in her behind! I wanted to meet her, but not that way.

By this time the laughter from all the people shut out the sounds of the bean cans. As she turned and looked at the cart with no one there, her eyes scanned the chaos to see who the perpetrator was and found me spread face down on the floor against the bean cans. I smiled. She laughed. We met. The rest is history. I wouldn't recommend that method, but it worked for me.

Where to Meet Eligible People

Where do you go to meet eligible people? Does it just happen as in this case, or do you work at making it happen? Some feel you will meet the right person by happenstance. Others contend you need to be aggressive in looking for a potential partner. Keep in mind that the greater the number of people of the kind you would be interested in, the greater the possibilities. It's best to look for abundance.

I heard the story of a high school teacher who had turned 40. She suddenly realized she really wanted to be married. But being a teacher, she had neither time nor energy during the school year to look around, so during the summer this became her project. She used personal ads in singles' magazines and went to numerous events and activities that she enjoyed. For two summers she did this, and during that time she actually interviewed 68 men. She married the 68th.[42]

Working at this project is a much better possibility than waiting for that predestined individual who's just going to one day out of the blue fall into your lap. And for many of these examples that do "just happen," when you look back you find that there usually was some orchestration of time, place, and events that occurred. It is true that you need to pray. Seek God's will for your life—whether being married or remaining single—and then ask for His leading. But you just don't sit at home waiting for a knock on the door. It's a combination of praying, waiting, and looking.

I've talked to several people who grew up in small towns. They said they didn't want to move from their town, but since they didn't find someone in college, they figured it would be better to live in a large city for a while so they could spouse-hunt. There just weren't that many available attractive prospects for them in a town of 4000.

This may sound simplistic to say, but it needs to be said, and you'll see why later. If you're interested in marriage and interested in a certain person, is that candidate available? You may be interested, attracted, head-over-heels in love, but if they're not available, your efforts will be unrewarded. There are some people who are available and others who aren't.

Availability—
Psychological and Situational

There are two kinds of availability, psychological and situational. Psychological availability includes having recovered and grown from previous relationships, having separated emotionally from parents in a healthy way, having the ability to commit to another person, and not being afraid of marriage.

Situational availability includes several factors. If the person you are interested in is living with a lover, not only are they not a good choice for you emotionally and spiritually, the fact that they haven't chosen marriage is another warning sign. Why didn't they marry? What about their relationship with the Lord? If they have just come out of a "living together" arrangement, the same concerns on your part need to be there. This person is not a good candidate now. Give them a couple of years to grow spiritually and emotionally.

If you're interested in someone who is separated, they aren't available. They're still married in the eyes of the state and God, whether the separation has been five weeks or five years. Aside from that, what a person goes through emotionally during the breakup of a marriage means they are not at all ready for a new relationship, even though they may be desperate for one.

A divorced person is a possibility depending upon how long it's been, financial status, bitterness, emotional readiness, etc.

There is one other category to consider: those who are married . . . to their work or to their family of origin. There are many others who are available. You can find them, but just keep these considerations in mind.[43]

Where to Begin Looking

Where does a person begin? Look around you. Where do you live? In an apartment complex? If so, what kind of get-togethers do they have? If they have some, are they the kind you're comfortable with or are they too wild? Why not create your own? I've seen groups started in companies and apartments for Christian singles' Bible studies as well as social events. If you can find two or three others, all of you could work toward this goal by sending out information.

In a one-mile radius around your home, what are the stores, the shops, the entertainment possibilities? Do you ever walk or jog in your neighborhood either on the sidewalks or at a school facility? *Remember a key factor*: Put yourself in a place where you're most likely to find the person that fits your most-wanted list! We'll come back to this point again and again. Will the places suggested here meet this factor? That's for you to decide.

Sometimes having some assistance helps you meet others, whether walking in a residential area, at an outdoor mall, on the beach, or anyplace near you where there are people. What am I talking about? Several years ago we got a golden retriever. I have walked him all over the place, including every local spot mentioned above. Because of the striking appearance and outgoing personality of Sheffield (my dog), my wife and I have met dozens of people we probably never would have otherwise. Our dog acts as a magnet and draws people of all ages. Then he becomes the point of contact and friendships even on the block where we've lived for almost a quarter of a century!

Speaking of dogs, a friend of mine used to take his Labrador puppy to the beach with him. One day he noticed a very attractive woman standing by the water in a two-piece bathing suit. As he sat there watching her, he began to mull over how he could meet her. But while he was thinking, his dog took matters into his own hands. The dog headed toward the water, angled toward the woman, and when he arrived proceeded to hike his hind leg and relieve himself on her leg. She was not too happy about this turn of events. There are better and safer ways for an introduction.

Another place to meet possible partners is at work or work-related activities. This occurs through the process of networking.

Some people don't like to have friends or relatives either suggest a possible partner or introduce them to someone. Sometimes other people can be very intrusive into our lives, especially when they are pushy and incessant. They make statements like, "I just know that the two of you will hit it off" or "This is the perfect one for you" or "I've told him all about you and he can't wait to meet you." As if they're experts on you! When you hear comments like the first two statements, you might shift the responsibility back to them and respond with, "Tell me why you think we'll hit it off." You could also say, "I appreciate your thinking about me in this way and I'll consider this possibility. You realize, though, it may not work out for some reason. And if so, you probably won't know why. Is that all right with you?"

Some of you may want this assistance from other people. If you do, don't leave it up to random selection on the part of those on your search committee. Why not create a "wanted" poster giving a description of the type of person you're seeking. Give your friends some guidance to go by, and it will save you some time. My wife and I have a friend who is in her thirties. We have introduced her to several Christian men, one of whom she dated for a while. She was appreciative of the help, even though at the time of this writing we're still looking.

My daughter married at the age of 27 after two previous engagements. She was a manicurist at a hair and nail salon. One day when she went to work she walked in and glanced over at one of her Christian friends who was in the process of cutting a young man's hair. She noticed they were both staring at her, so she walked over to them and said, "What's going on?" The young man looked at her and said, "We've just been talking about you." The hairdresser said, "Yes, I have been telling Bill that he needs to take you out on a date since you don't have any weird diseases." Sheryl said she turned red! They laughed and chatted a bit more. After he left, Sheryl took Jan in the back room and asked who he was. Jan told her that she'd been cutting his hair for the past four years, he was a Christian, and needed to have a date with her. Sheryl told her to give him her phone number, and the rest is history. They were married in 1988. Something like this could work for you.

There are times in the counseling office when a person will say, "Where do I go to meet people?" I have two stock questions to ask in reply: "What do you enjoy doing?" and "What would you enjoy doing with a marriage partner?" Go to those places that would give you things in common with the person you marry. If you're into art, visit galleries and exhibits. Consider bookstores, libraries, swap meets, video stores—or even the Laundromat. One writer suggested that women go to supermarkets early in the evening, since men tend to shop earlier. And when you go to the Laundromat, take extra bleach and fabric softener since men tend to forget these items!

If you're a real time-saver or time-oriented person, what I'm going to suggest may stress you somewhat. I know that many busy people try to hit stores or even sports clubs when they are least crowded. But that won't work when you're trying to meet others. Go at the *busiest* time, since there are more people there, especially in the Laundromat. And above all, talk to people. Take a book with you, but not to read. If you're hoping to meet a Christian, take a Christian-oriented book with you or wear something with a distinctively Christian message on it. Both of these attract attention and are discussion-starters.

A Christian man or woman has a much smaller pool of possibilities to choose from, so it's important to find places or events where other Christians gather. You may either live in an area which is limited in population or attend a church that is quite small. It could be there are no singles' groups in your own church or even in your area. You may out of necessity be the person who could assist in developing such a group. Singles' conferences, both regional and local, can be a source of contact. If your church doesn't have a ministry to singles, begin calling other churches. In larger metropolitan areas there are numerous churches which have well-developed programs for singles, and those who attend are not just from that local church. They come from dozens of other churches just for the opportunity to be ministered to and to meet people. There is nothing wrong in looking to church singles' groups to meet a prospective partner. That's part of the purpose of these groups.

One husband who had been married for 33 years shared with me how he met his wife at a church. Through college he had dated, but hadn't found anyone. Now that he was out of the college department at his church and moving into business, he decided he wanted to get married. He said, "I was spiritually immature at that time, so I put out a ten-minute fleece to the Lord about finding a wife. I was sitting in church when I said, 'Lord after this service, I'm going to go down to the college department, and if there is a woman there to be my wife, have her walk toward me.' I went down to the college department and started looking over the women there row by row. It was a cross between Death Valley and the Dead Sea. I was getting discouraged when I saw this woman walking away from me. All I could see was her back, but I knew she was a real possibility. I met her, and six weeks later we were engaged."

Dating and Dating Services

I've heard a number of people in their thirties and forties comment on the negative experiences they've had dating. It's expensive and a waste of time investing in someone and then not having it work out, and it's difficult to juggle dating when you're working and have kids.

Dating is a problem. But in spite of the negatives, consider what happens in dating. In dating you will discover what either attracts you to a person or repulses ... or a combination of both.

In dating, if you are seeing someone who is not bringing out the best in you, there's a message there for you to hear: Stop dating them.

In dating you're taking a big risk. It's called the possibility of rejection. But it's worth it. If it happens, it's not, I repeat, *not* because you're defective!

In dating you could become so enamored and infatuated that you think your partner can do little that is wrong. But eventually the bubble will burst, and the sooner the better so you can now build a real relationship. Without dating this may not have happened.

In dating the purpose is to discover if you and this other person can build a relationship, perhaps permanent. And if not, it still hasn't been time wasted.

Christian dating services have become more and more popular over the years. I know that there are many jokes about using such a service and you don't always know about some of the people who join, but it appears there are more benefits than negatives. I've interviewed numerous singles who have been involved with these services, and they felt that overall they were beneficial. Before using any such service, though, investigate it thoroughly. Find out about the history of the service, the population sample it has or number of participants. Basically this program is a networking service allowing singles to contact people who may have similar interests.

Perhaps Southern California is unusual in the variety of dating services available. One such program is called Equally Yoked. This is what their brochure states:

> *Choosing a lifetime mate to share a Christ-centered marriage is the most important decision Christians will make!*

> *Equally Yoked* Christian Introductions has served thousands of Christian singles since 1986, and the Lord has blessed over 250 members with husbands and wives. We offer this service because, other than church, there aren't many opportunities for single Christians to meet. Even pastors have met their wives through our service.

> **Personal Screening.** *Equally Yoked* meets each of our new members face-to-face and discusses their Christian testimony. Prospective members provide spiritual and personal references upon request.

> **How does it work?** Each member completes a profile sheet, submits pictures, and answers five interview-style questions, including their Christian testimony on a brief video. Our mutual consent selection process ensures both members would like to meet each other. *Equally Yoked* is simply a means of providing Christian singles exposure.

Equally Yoked today now has six offices serving Southern California (Redondo Beach and Ventura opened in May) and is expanding nationally! All *Equally Yoked* staff are committed Christians and dedicated to provide excellent service to our membership. Please call your nearest office for your free orientation.[44]

Another is called Christian Singles Connection—a ministry to the unmarried Christian in the body of Christ. The bimonthly publication that I saw contained over a thousand advertisements of men looking for women and women looking for men. The paper begins with the statement: "Christian Datemate Connections—for Friendships. Fellowship. Dating. Marriage." This is a nationwide organization for Protestants, Catholics, and Messianic Jews. Their statement of purpose reads:

Acting On Your Faith

Most of us have gone through the experience of searching for a job at one time or another. We check the want ads, send resumes, go to interviews and do everything in our power to find the job we need. But most of all we pray, trusting God to lead us into the right job at the right time. No one would suggest that by actively searching we fail to rely on God. Yet occasionally we talk with single Christians who feel that to actively search out a partner would be showing a lack of faith. However, in Genesis 24, Abraham, unable to find a suitable wife for his son in the land of the Canaanites, sent a servant to the Hebrews with orders to find a suitable wife. Abraham did everything he could to increase his son's opportunities to find the kind of mate God wanted him to have.

By initiating the search, he was acting on that faith. So it is with single Christians today. To find our chosen mates we must step out in faith and allow God to lead us. God can not lead us if we're not moving. God tells us in His Word that we are not to be unequally yoked with unbelievers. Through our Christian Datemate service, you will greatly expand your opportunities to connect with Christians in your area whether it be for friendships, dating relationships, or the possibility of marriage![45]

It is possible to contact the person by voicemail or through a letter. The ads that you read in chapter 4 were taken from this paper. This program also gives a listing of singles' activities and events for social gatherings.

A third program has the following as its statement of purpose and philosophy:

Christian Singles Confidential Introductions
Southern California's Exclusively Christian Single
One-On-One Personal Introduction Service
Since 1987

Christian Love Is Not Lacking In The World— Only Finding It. The world is filled with God's believers wanting to "give" and "receive" love. Christian Singles Confidential Introductions was formed as a nondenominational ministry that God can use as a means to help provide a way for Christians, who love the Lord, **to find each other.**

Finding A Christian Mate In This Complex Society Can Sometimes Be Difficult. Studies indicate chance encounters are limited and a lot of years wasted. Christian Singles Confidential Introductions was created for those who would like to use a Christian introduction service, *but are concerned* *about privacy and confidentiality,* not being comfortable using a 900 number, the personals, or recording a video for others to view.

If You Are *Seriously* **Seeking A Christian Lifetime Mate** and would prefer a more confidential way of finding a *"compatible"* Christian mate, Christian Singles Confidential Introductions is a caring, very confidential, one-on-one personalized service of exclusive Christian singles. CSCI is not a video dating service, *you are introduced to each person individually.*

A Recent Los Angeles Times Poll Sampled Opinions Of Over 2,000 Single Adults. The most popular answer to their main goal was "To Be Happily Married"! **This Is Because God Created You With A Need For Another Person.**

God's Word Very Clearly States In 2 Corinthians 6:14-18, Christians Should Marry Only Other Christians. If you cannot find a compatible Christian to date, you will eventually—out of loneliness—date non-Christians. *If you continue to date non-Christians, you will eventually marry a non-Christian.*

My Heart's Desire Is To Help Insure You A More Successful Marriage By Finding You:

1. Someone Who Loves The Lord As You Do. **According To God's Word This Is Number One.**

2. Someone You Can Like And Become Your Best Friend, **Then Love.**

3. Someone **Who Is A Lot Like You** (In Other Words Compatible) With Similar Interests. **Every Common Interest You Have Is A Blessing.** Some Minor Incompatibilities Can Be Overcome, However, Some Are **Absolutely**

Essential Like Spirituality, Energy Level, Money Use, Personal Habits.

4. Someone Who Has The Magic Ingredient You Need To Begin A Relationship—**Chemistry.** Physical Attraction Is Critical, **However Should Not Be The Sole Criteria.**

5. Someone Who Is Emotionally Healthy **Before** Marriage As Stated In Philippians Chapter 3 Verse 13: **"Bringing All Your Energies To Bear On One Thing. Forgetting The Past And Looking Forward To The Future."**

6. Someone Having The Same Goals—**Not Letting Weeds Grow Around "Your" Dreams.** People Who Are Truly In Love And Are Compatible, Will Have The Same Shared Dreams And Goals To Reach Them.

7. Someone With Whom You Can Communicate Emotionally—Who Has A Desire To Share Intimacy (Not Relating Only To Sex) **But The Sharing Of Emotions, Thoughts, Feelings, Fears and Joys.**

8. Someone You Can Be Comfortable With, **So You Can Be Yourself.** Someone **Genuine** Who Does Not Play Games By Having A Facade During The Courtship **And Does Not Portray Who They Really Are.**[46]

This ministry is highly confidential, is not designed to be a dating service, but wants to match compatible Christian couples for lifetime commitment. The personal application to be filled out is very detailed, and a three-hour personal interview by the founder of this ministry is involved. (The addresses for these three ministries are in the notes for this chapter.)

If you use a service such as these and are interested in meeting someone, be sure to use the GASP approach. Translated, it means the first and perhaps several initial contacts are *Get Acquainted Sessions* and not to be considered as dates. Use the time for investigation rather than selection. That can come later. You need to discover as much as you can about this individual and develop just a friendship first. Let the romantic side develop from being friends.

As with any program or ministry, screening is very important. People do misrepresent themselves, and the ads placed are for the purpose of making contact. Make your first contacts over the *Phone* initially, and the hours spent may help you determine if you want to get together or not. You don't want to end up feeling stuck and obligated with a person for several hours.

A male friend shared his reflections on several years of dating and using such services. I believe his experience can be helpful to anyone dating.

> In searching for the perfect mate, it has taken a long time for me to discover that there really is no such creature out there. Everything is found in degrees of compromise—Can I live with this or can I accept that, etc. Then when I have found one that fits most all of my criteria and parameters, then the question is "Will I fit hers?" It's extremely difficult trying to find someone where the gears all seem to mesh into place without a lot of grinding.

> I think one of the more important things that I find invaluable in dating now is all the experience that I have compiled over the years. Having years of different situations, I have reached the point now in my 40's where I feel that I finally know some of the answers to the questions that I didn't even know to ask in my 20's or 30's. But even now I am still adding and updating my list of questions.

If there are any bits of advice that I could give anyone that is looking for the ideal mate for themselves it is this: Ask questions of anyone you date and store their answers in your memory bank to see if the answers continue to be consistent with their actions. If something appears to be a red flag, confront it and don't let it slide as "It's not that big of a deal." Interact with the other person's friends (in group settings) such as on camping trips or skiing trips or play interaction group type games. If possible spend time with the other person's parents (and if there are any red flags, don't ignore them, because *their child is a product of their environment*). If there are ways of seeing how the other person will handle pressure situations...put them in it (this way you are able to see how flexible they are or can be and how they will hold up under pressure), build a real friendship but stay out of bed, pray together, have similar values and interests in things, come to know the other person's faults and know that you can accept them, watch to see how they treat their pets, and continue to interview right up to the last moments before marriage....

And as hard as it may seem, if that inner voice from within tells you that you are making a mistake, at least stop and listen to it and be willing to pull the plug or at least put it on hold until things can be clarified in the relationship right up to the day of the wedding. It is my feelings that I would much rather be very embarrassed and cause hurt to both of us by putting things on hold or having to walk away from the relationship right up to the final days before the wedding, than suck it up, be a man and live in misery for the rest of my life. Why marry when maybe in reality you knew deep down inside of you that things were not right or small things were adding up to be big things but you didn't know how to confront them or you were afraid that you might hurt the other person by confronting her. A lot of this stuff will come to the surface through premarital counseling. Know ahead of time that some people are able to mask or hide things or if you don't ask specific questions may feel that "If you didn't ask, they didn't lie."

As I look back in my dating over the years, I have come to realize how really naive I was in even trying to find out what questions I should ask or thinking that I really didn't have the right to be asking certain questions until I was further into the relationship. There were some questions of which it didn't even occur to me that I would have to ask a "Christian." I assumed that she would have never have been into something that would be blatantly wrong that you would have to ask. *Never assume anything!* I now have a list of about twelve questions that I ask right from the beginning, and if they have problems with it, I would rather know now and save myself from becoming involved and the additional hurt from having to break up later. These are questions that I would feel comfortable answering for someone who was interested in dating me.

Even though in the past I have asked questions, I found that my list of questions was not complete (and I will continually be adding things to the list as experience dictates). A good example of this was recently, I met a woman that enjoyed a number of activities that I did and she *claimed* to be a Christian. After a number of dates we found that we were enjoying each other, and she invited me to go along with her and a group of her Christian friends to the mountains for a fishing trip. I found this setting absolutely invaluable for insights that I didn't see while we were dating one on one. First I saw that her language changed when she was with her friends. Plus, she became more worldly in this atmosphere (flags started popping up). She then went into depression and wouldn't open up to what the problem was. Then when everybody was ready to go out for afternoon fishing, she decided that she wanted to go shopping instead of fishing. She talked one of her girlfriends into going along with her, which was fine. However, she and her girlfriend didn't get back for dinner until 9 P.M.— drunk. Instead of going shopping, they went to the local mountain cowboy bar to go dancing and drinking. All that I could think of was "Thank you, Lord, for opening my eyes now."

A week later, she dropped by and proudly showed me an engagement ring. She let me know that the reason she acted the way she did on the trip was because she found that she was missing this great "Christian" guy that she had been living with for the past year and a half. She had forgotten to mention it when we had started dating. The fact that she had just broken up with him a few weeks earlier had slipped her mind. As I looked over my list of questions, I really thought that asking a "Christian" if they had been living with someone since they had become a "Christian" really wasn't necessary, but rather an oxymoron. Like I said before, NEVER ASSUME.

A friend of mine spends hours talking about everything including family background, vocation, interests, sports, friendship, their Christian faith, desire for children, sexual standards, and boundaries. After several conversations, then the decision to get together is made. Friends have given me the list of questions they use for their phone interview (see Appendix A).

Sometimes the contacts are just by mail. Here is an example of a letter written by a man to a response inquiry to his ad. The woman writing had given a general description and background of herself as well as a picture.

Dear Jean,

Thank you for your recent letter and for answering my ad in CSC. You probably, like myself, have found it difficult meeting quality Christians that have some of the same values and interests as yourself, so thank you for taking a chance.

Please let me introduce myself to you, my name is John Smith, I am the one that "loves the outdoors."

I'm 48 years old, young at heart and try to keep myself physically fit through playing racquetball twice a week and working out on other days. I play tennis whenever I can find a partner (and yes, I am patient) and I enjoy hiking, mountain bike riding and jogging through the hills behind my house when they don't have it closed down from being a fire hazard.

But what I really enjoy is being out in the outdoors, loving to fish, camp, travel, horseback ride, boat and water ski (along with jet skiing) and snow skiing. I equally enjoy both mountains and beach. When I have a chance, I love to fish Baja, Mexico (where the water is calm and you won't turn *too* blue) in the winters and then stay in a friend's cottage, on a small island in BC, Canada in the summers. When time allows I like to travel and camp through Utah, Wyoming and Montana, sometimes wondering which of these beautiful places that I would like to live if I had a chance. It's kind of fun to daydream!

Professionally, I'm in the travel marketing business, where I represent lodges, resorts, hotels, airlines, B&B's, and guest ranches to travel trade shows for travel agents, distributing their literature and brochures to the agents. I have also been involved with putting on a Sports, Vacation and RV Show at Convention Centers for the past 14 years.

I've been attending the First Evangelical Free Church of Fullerton for the past 20 years and feel that I have really learned and benefited from Chuck Swindoll's teachings and insights. I'm going to really miss him, now that he has gone to Dallas Theological Seminary to be the school's president.

Jean, you asked if I have had any luck with the ad so far? Well, yes and no. I have met some very wonderful ladies through this (but, unfortunately gears just never meshed) and I have had some horrible experiences, where the dates had totally misrepresented themselves. So, as a result I have found that I now not only ask for a picture (as yes, I am a normal, visual male and would like to see if I am going to be attracted towards the other person, and no, I am not looking for perfection, as it does not exist, male or female) but also have a list of questions that I have found necessary to ask not only just to see if there is enough substance in addition to having like interests and being attracted by a picture, but having similar values and beliefs are also very important to me.

I am not dating just to be dating, and with some of the experiences that I have had, I didn't think that you would have to ask a Christian some of these questions, but I was wrong. I have found that I should not take anything for granted. So, if you wouldn't mind along with sending a photo of yourself (and if you do and this part doesn't scare you off and you would care to pursue this further), please answer the following questions:

1) Have you ever been married, if so for how long?
2) Is your divorce final and when was it final?
3) How many times have you been married (including any annulments)?
4) Do you have any children and do they live with you?
5) Have you ever been involved in a relationship with a woman?
6) Have you, since being a Christian, lived with a guy?
7) Are you Charismatic?
8) Are you Democrat, Republican or Independent?
9) Are you pre-tribulation, post-tribulation, or neither?
10) To you, what are the five most important qualities that you want and look for in a mate (in order of importance)?
11) Do you smoke or use drugs?
12) And finally, who is Jesus to you and what does He mean to you in your life?

It might not sound like it here, but I really am a fun guy and enjoy having a good time, but have had to become more cautious (through experience) in my dating through the mail. I hope that I haven't offended or blown you away in any way, but since you are new at this type of dating you might think of asking some of these questions or some of your own, as it could sure save you a lot of time and heartbreaks. And feel free to ask any questions of me if you like, as I am a pretty open person.

Look forward to hearing from you.

God Bless,

John Smith

When you do get together the first time, don't commit yourself to an extended period of time. Plan a one-hour, two-hour, or three-hour get-together. Once you've met and seem to hit it off, then you may want to expand your time. And doing it this way can help to avoid expensive get-togethers.

For the initial contact meet one another at a neutral site. By doing this you are making it safer. There are both men and women who would prefer not having the new person know where they live initially until they are better acquainted. Meet at a coffee shop or someplace where you can talk and interact. Going to a play, movie, or even a church service is not going to help you get acquainted.

Several times I've heard singles say, "I messed up bad the first time I talked with him or her. I guess I was so anxious to make a good impression, I became tongue-tied. I'm sure they thought something was wrong with me." Perhaps the problem that creates stress is looking at this individual as a possible spouse. Don't. You don't know them yet. You're just getting acquainted with another stranger. You don't know if you're going to like the person or not. Trying to impress them won't work. Just be yourself and carry on a conversation just like you would with anyone else. And in time you'll never know where you will meet someone or how it will turn out.

We've all heard the horror stories of how relationships didn't work out. Consider this one that did succeed from the initial date through the first 11 years of marriage:

THE MEETING & DATING

I was 18 and in my first year of college. In January at the beginning of the new semester, we had a new student, a male. I am, by nature, somewhat friendly and outgoing, so most of the girls in this very small class, began to ask me who "the new guy" was. No one knew and no one was finding out, so I boldly walked over to the guy and said, "Hi, who are you?" He told me his name and I shared mine. I then proceeded to introduce him to the other students in the class. . . .

THE ATTRACTION

At the time I met Mark, I was headed "for trouble" (I was dating guys I shouldn't be). Mark is old-fashioned and immediately began treating me "like a lady." Opening and closing my car door, making sure my coat was all the way in the car (and not half out the door!). He treated me with such respect. Plus, he was attractive and had a little money to go out. All very attractive qualities to me! He also seemed to have a strong relationship with the Lord.

Mark came from a very quiet traditional reserved family that showed little emotion. I came from a very noisy boisterous family—one who had a lot of love and affection, and showed it! The kind that had mom and dad kissing in the kitchen when we kids came home from wherever. I suppose that this freedom of speech and freedom of hugs and kisses was attractive to Mark as well as the support of his person. I guess I could also say I have some "looks," which would be attractive to him, but that would be putting words into his mouth. . . .
One way to describe the differences in our families would be the story of when we went to visit our

sisters. Mark and I decided to take a trip to visit his sister for a day and then mine. They lived 45 minutes apart. We had "Sunday Dinner" at his sister's house complete with linen napkins and tablecloth, roast, potatoes, quiet table talk. Everyone passed all the food before the first bite was taken; and a lovely blessing of the food was said. Then we had Sunday supper at my sister's house, complete with paper plates and napkins, lots of noise (both families had children), forgetting to pass the food (just help yourself), fried chicken to eat with your fingers, and a simple "Thanks God for the food" prayer. I thought it was quite funny to have the differences so contrasted. We have since discovered, that is a very accurate picture of each of us. Mark is quiet and reserved, and I am noisy and outgoing. We are very opposite!

THE PROPOSAL

About 6 months before Mark proposed, we began talking about which direction our relationship was headed. At that point we had been dating 2 years. Our question was whether we felt God wanted us to be together. (We didn't want to date for many years, just to find we weren't supposed to be together.) So, we decided that we would begin earnestly seeking what God wanted and we would either break up or get engaged! We had been having a long-distance relationship for approximately one year—he was away at school. We decided the decision would be made before he went back to school in September. I had felt as if God told me early in the relationship that he was the one I was supposed to marry. (I think I needed to know that, otherwise I probably would have broken up with him soon after we began dating.) Since I didn't know what God was saying to him, I didn't want to push. September came and went, no decision. Then we were to decide by Thanksgiving, then Christmas, and then before he went back to school in January. I began to be concerned that Mark was leaning toward breaking up, and if he did then I figured God had another plan for me. Finally the last day came before he was to leave for school. We decided to go out for dinner. Dinner ended, the restaurant was closed, the workers were mopping the floor when Mark decided we should discuss the pros and cons of whether or not to get married! For every pro I brought up, he brought up a con. I began to get frustrated when he finally listed some more pros. He then said, "I feel confident by looking at this, that you can fill the job" (or something close to that). My reply (knowing what he meant, but still somewhat frustrated) was "What are you asking?" "I'm asking you to be my wife, will you marry me?" I told him that with my father's permission, I would. (Hallelujah! He finally did it!) We went home about 10:30 P.M. and began the process of calling our parents. Mine lived in Arkansas. So, when we called them, it was close to 1:00 A.M. Mom had always said that if I got engaged, I was to call collect, so I was sure that she would know why I was calling collect at 1:00 A.M. Needless to say, our parents were thrilled.

THE WEDDING

Our wedding was the day I had always planned for (with the exception of the flower girl picking her nose!). My goal for the day was that the focus would be on God. We had a lovely ceremony with lots of music—as my family loves music (we grew up playing instruments and singing often with 3 generations taking part!). My sibling participated in singing most of the songs. Our ceremony was planned around the fact that God is the center of our lives AND the center of our marriage.

There are many stories like this. Take the time to search for a person, screen them carefully, and then select.

Relationships: Short-term, Long-term, and None

ou've met someone who's a real possibility. You're interested and they're interested. You don't know where this could go, but you're willing to pursue it. You just met and spent a few minutes talking, and there's a definite interest . . . on both sides. This could become, well, think of all the possibilities—a friendship, a short-term romance or maybe long-term, maybe even marriage. Who knows?

What Are You Looking For?

Have you considered letting people know what you are looking for right up front? It's possible, and it can save you and the other person some time and even heartache. Now and then you will find an expression of this in one of the dating ads. Some come right out and say, "Looking for romance, commitment, and eventually marriage," or "Just want to date and see what happens," or "Not interested in marriage, but a good friend." Perhaps more of this needs to occur right up front.

The initial step is to determine what you are ultimately looking for in your relationship endeavors. Some men and women have said they let it be known the first time they're together with a new person what their long-range goals are. Then as soon as possible, they try to discover what the other person is seeking. Everyone has some kind of plans or preferences. One way to draw someone out is to share your own. If you're looking for a marriage partner and this new person isn't, why waste your time? If they indicate they are, too, but for the past 12 years they've had one series of six-month relationships after another, what does that tell you? You hope you'll be the answer to their searching, but that's a high risk. A person's relationship history may have a message for you, too.

Here's what a 33-year-old woman shared as her criteria:

What I look for in a godly man

Spirituality is the umbrella, and then there are things under that. If the umbrella isn't there, I don't care what the outer appearances of the guy are: he might be a looker, a charmer, quite a talker, a doer, a go-getter; however, if the evidences of a strong walk with the Lord are not there, I am not interested.

However, once under the umbrella, qualities I find attractive are as follows:

—A person of whom my parents approve (particularly my father);

—A person who is trustworthy;

—A person of integrity (His word is his bond—when he says something, I feel confident it is going to be done. When he says something, I know he is going to do it).

—Someone I can look up to—a person I would like to emulate.

—Someone that's courteous—not one that will put me down.

—A good listener.

—A supportive person—we might disagree on some things, but he would listen to my point before making a decision about right or wrong.

—A good communicator. While I understand we won't always agree on things or have the same opinion of things, I want someone who at least *tries* to understand and communicate with me. This is one of the more important qualities for which I look.

The idea of integrity comes back to mind—in all facets of his being. Integrity toward his God, his spouse, his employer, his friends, his finances (the church, the IRS, etc.) and to himself. Does he try to convince himself of something that just isn't the case?

Most of this rather "strict" approach to looking for a godly man is for two reasons: One is that I am a Christian and the thought of being with an unbeliever is not only repelling, it also is against God's will. The other reason is because I tried it the other way and I *know* how unhappy (actually, downright miserable) I was. I knew I was involved in relationships which weren't the ideal, but I didn't know how to extricate myself from some of the destructive relationships in which I was.

With respect to *dating*, ideally I won't actually date. In other words, I would like to get to know the godly man as a friend. I would like for kissing, etc. not to be an issue. I truly believe that I could meet someone and get to know him on an intellectual and spiritual level and know at that point whether I wanted to marry him. The physical aspect of a relationship doesn't have to be part of the courtship I have with a person. I have enough faith and belief in God that He will work out the physical aspects of our relationship.

Consequently, ideas that feel right or comfortable to me are to meet someone in groups of other Christians (either in a Sunday school class or in church, or in some outreach project). I would like to get to know him in groups—at least initially—before having any one-on-one time.

Lastly, and yet *most importantly*, having come through the background I have, I absolutely believe and know that prayer in a relationship is essential. In fact, it is prayer which will allow God to let me know His will about a particular man in my life. Additionally, praying together is something which will be a must for me.

Some individuals are quite satisfied and fulfilled with short-term relationships. This has been their pattern over the years and they are not pressing for marriage. Sometimes those in constant and frequent short-term relationships project the reason for this onto their partners. They say, "She just didn't seem interested in marriage" or "He wasn't the commitment type. Few men are these days." People who follow this pattern of relationships usually have a high or "peak" intensity of attraction at the beginning, but over the next few months it diminishes. The relationship feels good and often there is intense passion. It's as though there is an addictive chemical at work, but it rarely lasts. You can't always explain why you are drawn to this person and sometimes who and what they are fails to match up to your qualifications list.

Infatuation does not have to have a correlation with reality. Infatuation/passion is so common with adolescents, and yet it can become a continuous pattern for adults in their twenties and thirties as well. Unfortunately, when the IP (infatuation/passion) fails to occur immediately, the person may not seem interested in pursuing the possibilities.

There is possibly more hope for a relationship developing and lasting without infatuation than with the IP pattern. As a couple dates and the intensity begins to subside, it creates a possibility for necessary evaluation of the relationship and the other person, as well as the opportunity for mature love to develop. If some crisis occurs to make you look at the relationship in a new way, so much the better. This is positive, for this is life. When you encounter a crisis together, you are able to see another often hidden side of the other individual. We are more willing to make changes during some of the crises.

When couples who are in pre-engagement or pre-marital counseling come in and state they had a difficult week or experienced major upsets, my response is "Wonderful, we'll be able to accomplish more this week. We can use what happened to determine the effect upon your relationship. This is positive." They don't usually see it that way, but in time they will see the benefits. Or if a couple doesn't experience very much upset during the weeks we spend together, I bring up issues and subjects that may cause serious discussion, reevaluation, or even conflict. This is what life is like when you're married. Before you marry is when you need to discover if you can really handle the issues.

When you enter a time of reevaluating a relationship to determine whether you will move forward or dissolve it, you will probably consider numerous questions. Do you want to continue this relationship, and if so, in what way? Are you content to maintain at this level, or do you want to work to move it to a deeper and perhaps lasting relationship? Are you capable at this time of making such a decision? Are you capable of sharing whatever your feelings are for the person for a lifetime? Are you considering staying in this relationship for a positive reason, or because it's better than being alone until something better comes along? These are questions to think about early on in a relationship.

Perhaps one of the questions for you to consider as you begin becoming acquainted with a person is, "Does this relationship have long-lasting potential?" Ask yourself this question, and rate it on a scale of 1 to 10 (1 being "forget it" and 10 being "absolutely yes"). Do this each time you see the person and spend time with him/her. Keep track of this for a month and then ask yourself the question, "What are these results telling me?" To assist you in getting to know a person better, you may want to use the interview questions suggested in Appendix A.

Concerns About a Long-Term Relationship

Often I request that my counselees respond to questions during the week in writing. I've discovered that when we see our written response it has more of an impact. For a person involved in a pattern of short-term relationships or for someone desiring a long-term relationship, it may be beneficial to reflect on your concerns of moving ahead. List five of your concerns and then rate their intensity on a scale of 1 to 5.

<u>My Concerns About a Long-Term Relationship Are . . .</u>

1.

2.

3.

4.

5.

Now consider some of these concerns that other singles have voiced.

—What if I'm just fulfilling the other person's needs rather than my own?

—I'm not sure if we continue that the level of giving to him is reciprocated. I'd like it to be two-way.

—It's been difficult so far. How do I know it will be any better? I'd like to be closer, but I don't want to lose my independence, either.

—If we continue in the relationship, she may find other things she doesn't like about me. I could be rejected big time if I'm more attached to her than I am now. I want closeness, but not at the risk of the pain of rejection. I've experienced that before.

—He tends to be so strong. If we continue the relationship I could end up being dominated.

—I know I'm strong and tend to be controlling. In a short-term relationship I can put a lid on it fairly well. But the longer I go with someone the harder it is, especially when I see things that need to be corrected.

—If I become exclusively involved with someone, it's costly. I have to give up some of my activities as well as opposite-sex friends. Some have been friends for years.

—So I'm picky. I know it. That's what keeps me from getting serious. I could miss out on someone else who is interesting.

Rebounders

Warning: There are two types of situations which are definitely hazardous to the health of a future marriage. You've heard about one of them before, especially if you're a basketball fan. In fact in this sport it is to a team's advantage to have players who excel in this particular skill. It's called *rebounding*. A basketball is shot toward the basket, but it bounces off the rim and an opposing player leaps high into the air and grabs the rebound so his team can have possession and now move toward their goal.

Catching the rebound in basketball is positive. Catching a person on the rebound is not! I see it all the time. A dating relationship is broken or a marriage is broken because of death or divorce, and very soon the person is involved with a new person. Often the rebounder is in intense pain over their loss and instead of experiencing the loss and grief on their own, they attempt to cover some of the pain by attaching to a new person in their life. The positive feelings are much more positive than the ache of the empty place in their life. In a sense, the other person is being used as an anesthetic by the rebounder to numb some of their hurt. You may be healthy and able to commit to a relationship at this time, but they aren't there yet. Rebounders enter into premature involvements which hinder them from healing and contaminate their new relationship. Both people need to be stable and healthy for a relationship to have a chance. [47]

If a person is now single because of the death of a spouse, was it a lingering, long-term terminal illness that led to the death? If so, there could have been a great deal of anticipatory grieving, and the person could recover much more rapidly following the death. But if not, it usually takes an average of two years for the grieving to occur after what we call natural death. But if it was an accidental death, it usually takes three years; suicide, four years; and death by homicide, usually five years. This is why grief-recovery groups are important before moving into a new relationship.

When a divorce occurs and the person is the rejected one, not only is there the loss of the relationship, but there is the pain of the rejection as well. Too often the person is moving into relationships before the divorce is even final. Numerous times men and women going through divorce have asked me if it's all right for them to date yet. I usually toss the question back to them by asking, "In the eyes of the state and God, are you single or married?" When they admit the truth (it may take awhile for this to occur), tell them, "If you're still married, then you're not eligible to date yet. Once you're divorced, attend and complete a divorce-recovery group. Then wait at least a year before even considering dating. You won't be ready until at least that time. If you get into relationships before that time, you're probably rebounding and looking for someone out of pain and need rather than from a healthy choice." Many counselees don't want to hear this. But those who remarry too soon are another divorce casualty waiting to happen.

Perhaps the kind of rebounding often found in broken relationships is best illustrated by throwing a racquetball against the wall of a small room in your home. It bounces erratically back and forth from wall to wall. One young woman described the process in my counseling office:

> I feel as though I'm on a combination merry-go-round, bumper car, and roller coaster all rolled up into one. I have to be on the go constantly or I think I'll go bananas. I'm always doing something and jumping into one relationship after another—and unfortunately, one bed after another. I don't like myself for doing this, and it makes me feel even worse about the relationship I lost. I've decided to find some more constructive things to do with my time and to stay home on Thursday and Friday night each week to prove that I'm able to do it. It hurts, but I think I'll recover by doing this and I'm sure I can grow through this experience. I don't want to be chained to him forever, and I think I have been.

Some may be ready for a relationship earlier than others, but you need to ask this question, "Am I being considered for who I am, a unique person they're interested in pursuing for me, or am I looked at as a cure?" The other question is, "Am I looking at the person I'm interested in as a cure, or am I regarding them for who they really are?"

How can you tell, though, if this new person in your life is a rebounder? First of all, before you invest too much time, discuss yours and his/her last relationship. If it was long-term, either dating or marriage, go into detail about the type of relationship, what caused the termination, how long ago, what he/she has done to recover, and how this person is doing in their adjustment. This is not being intrusive, but safe and practical. You may want to discover how similar or dissimilar you are to their former partner. I have seen many people choose men or women just like their former partners, defects and all. These replacements will probably be just as disappointing as the previous partners were. But something drives them to prove that they can have relationships with people like this. Perhaps it is to prove to themselves and their former partners that the defect wasn't in them. This is why many daughters who have nonaffirming, aloof, distant fathers choose husbands who are very much like their fathers. The similarities could be in personality characteristics, behavior, values, beliefs, etc.

Before any person can move ahead with a new relationship, it's necessary to say good-bye to the former person. It's the final step in the stages of grieving over a relationship. More will be said about this in a later chapter.

Rebounders tend to manifest certain characteristics, and if you see these in the other person, be cautious. If the other person has requests or demands which lead to major change in your life without your receiving need fulfillment, that's a warning sign. It could be a rebound symptom or an ingrained personality trait. In either case, it's not healthy for you.

Often rebounders use projection to ease the pain of their breakup. They heap blame upon their former partner and focus on his/her negative traits (which we all have). This tendency may keep them from seeing or assuming their part in the breakup. If they continue to bad-mouth their former partner as your relationship is building, they are still emotionally involved with the former partner, but with negative feelings. The anger which is there could lead to resentment, which can create a bitterness not just toward the original source, but perhaps to other people in their life and even you. You may want to discover who else they have blamed in their life for their misfortunes. You certainly don't want to be an addition in their trophy case of "bad guys."

Another way to numb yourself from the pain of the loss, especially if you were the one rejected, is to deny your former partner's good points. Statements such as these deaden the pain of the loss: "You know, that person really had a lot of problems and defects. She or he wasn't who or what they said they were. I'm better off in the long-run finding someone else."

Another question for you to consider is whether this person is the one who broke it off with his/her former partner or if he/she was the one rejected. In either case, has this been a pattern over the years? Where is their former partner now? Are they dating someone in a new relationship or married again? If so, am I the first person my new partner has had an interest in or have there been others? If you are the first one, why have they waited until now to pursue a new relationship?

Prebounders

There is a second type of situation that is hazardous to the health of a future marriage. I haven't known what to call it until recently. One author called them *prebounders*. They're very similar to the rebounder except they are still involved in their current relationship while they're looking for a new one. Once they are assured of a new partner, then they decide what to do about the present one. But who's to say that they might not give up the former relationship and keep two going at once? I've seen as many as five at one time. And if problems occur between the two of you, it's quite easy for them to return to their former partner. Now you're the one left out in the cold.

Here are some questions which would be helpful for you and your future if you know the honest answers. You may need to find creative ways to discuss them with your new interest. It's also vital that you answer them honestly for yourself. The questions pertain to "Is it really over?"

1. How frequently do you think about your former partner and in what way? Is it negative or positive?

2. How frequently do you have contact with your former partner and in what way? What is the purpose? What feelings do you experience on these occasions?

3. In what ways are you similar to this former partner?

4. On a scale of 0 to 10, to what extent do you have a fear that this past relationship may repeat itself again?

5. On a scale of 0 to 10, to what extent do you experience guilt over the previous relationship? How might this guilt be affecting you in building a relationship with another individual?

6. On a scale of 0 to 10, to what extent do you have anger toward the previous relationship? If there is anger, what can be done to resolve it?

I know. You may be thinking, "We could never discuss these." But at some time you can. Not only that, you need to. After all, it's your future. You will discover the answer one way or another. It can happen directly or in a way that could disrupt your relationship. If you are involved with a rebounder or prebounder, you're being used as a crutch. Keep in mind that when a broken leg heals, the crutch is discarded. It's something to consider.[48]

Think of it in this way. If you go to a new medical doctor, what does he do to help you? First, he takes a medical history with some questions that don't always seem to pertain to the ailment you brought to his attention. But in order to properly evaluate you, the doctor needs the total picture.

If you seek out a therapist for counseling, in some way or another you are asked to share your past history. A therapist wants to deal not only with the present problem, but also with how it developed and how it affects you. That way he can better help you.

Evaluating a potential mate isn't much different and is important for your future.

Before you consider moving into a possible long-term relationship with someone and possibly marriage, let's consider the "I don't need these kinds of problems" issues. If the problems are present at this time, you may want to consider them as either a caution or "stop the relationship" sign.

Givers, Takers, and Commitmentphobia

Years ago I read a book called *The Givers and The Takers*. It divided people into one of two camps. Ideally we have the ability to both give and receive. This is healthy. But if your partner is exclusively one or the other, you can count on one thing: Your needs won't be met.

If your partner uses threats of any kind to force you to continue to be involved with him or her such as violence, ruining your reputation, or suicide, you need to become uninvolved as soon as possible. Some individuals have difficulty accepting "no." (This topic will be discussed in greater depth in a later chapter.)

I am amazed at the number of married Christian couples who use the "D" word as a threat to control their partner. Threatening divorce is unhealthy in a marriage. If you have a partner who uses threats to get their way, you might consider showing them the door!

If your partner has a pattern of abusiveness in their background, how can you be sure that you won't experience this if they've never received help or treatment for it?

In the last two decades our English language has been inundated with many new labels in an attempt to explain relationships and problems in life. Many books are talking about one label that perhaps answers why some individuals never marry. The new villainous label in town is "commitmentphobia"! It's even been suggested we have an epidemic of this problem. It's especially painful for the partner in a relationship who deeply loves the other, but the partner cannot bring himself or herself to make a commitment. Numerous books discuss this problem, and usually the man is the culprit. A few titles are *The Dance-Away Lover, The Go-Away-Come-Closer Disease, The Playboy Syndrome, Flight from Commitment, The Peter Pan Syndrome,* and *Men Who Can't Love.*

A "commitmentphobic" is a person who has a strong, insatiable desire for affirmation from the opposite sex along with a resistance (a strong one at that) to commitment. They don't want to be alone, but they don't want to be too close. And just when they get too close, they retreat. Their double message is, "Come closer. Don't get too close. Come here. Go away." They're unhappy alone and unhappy if they're going to be tied down.

How do you detect commitmentphobics? If they have a history of short-term relationships, be aware. Do they cancel dates with you or change arrangements frequently? Do you find yourself being hurt by them? Do you see them settling down and changing their pattern? If not, be careful.

If for some reason you have a strong feeling you're involved with such a person, get out. Don't try to discover why he or she is like this or think you can change the individual. You won't and you can't. It's easy to fall into the trap of "I wonder why she canceled again?" or "I wonder why he's retreating?" You probably will never find out. Move on to someone with potential.

Another concern for the women are the committed bachelors. A newspaper carried an article with the title "Bachelor Fad" in which it stated that more and more men are choosing the single life rather than marriage. Many men do postpone marriage to pursue educational and career goals. The author of the book *Bachelors: The Psychology of Never-Married Men* found that many men didn't marry because it was their choice not to. The study revealed that many men shared three types of defenses in relationships: avoidance, isolation, and distortion. The single men appeared reluctant to become involved emotionally, make demands, or share their needs in sexual relationships. Their defensiveness and isolation allowed them to interact with women, but on a superficial level. Emotions were not shared. Overall their tendency was to be standoffish, indifferent. If there were any situations in which they might be hurt, avoidance was used. The surprising feature of this study according to the author was that only 5 percent of bachelors over 40 ever marry![49]

I've seen some strange combinations in premarital counseling. I've talked with couples who were going to be married where one of them didn't especially like the partner, but felt that wasn't necessary if physical needs were met. Another couple admitted they had a physical attraction to one another and financially they had similar goals, but they were not sure that they liked one another's personalities! Why would people even consider marriage with these liabilities? Yet they do. (Fortunately, the couples I mentioned eventually decided not to marry.)

Reasons for Continuing a Losing Relationship

Of the numerous problems mentioned in this chapter, think about them in this way: If there is an issue now, why wouldn't it be a problem after marriage and with greater intensity? If you can take the necessary steps to resolve the issues, that would be wonderful. But that will take time.[50]

Why would you want to continue a relationship when the problems are so obvious (perhaps even more so now after reading what you've read)? There are several reasons.

It could be a struggle with low self-esteem. One 40-year-old counselee described her dilemma with her boyfriend. She told about his constant put-downs which made her self-esteem crumble. I asked why she didn't break up the relationship, and she said "I would miss out on the companionship I have. I'd be uncomfortable starting over with someone else. And maybe his negative perceptions of me are accurate." If you hear negatives enough, you begin to believe them.

Some individuals seem to be ruled by their feelings regardless of the objective facts. I see those who spend their time in romance novels and in feeding their fantasy life about an intense romantic love relationship falling into this group. Sometimes what you fantasize about becomes so intense that it can override the reality that you are in, and you fail to notice the danger signals.

Obsessive Lovers

Some people are addicted to love, no matter what the consequences. In a healthy relationship you may hope and even idealize that perhaps you have found the person who may be the fulfillment of your hopes and dreams. But it's balanced with the realization that it may not work out. You have a safety net called reality. An obsessive lover works without a net and doesn't even understand the word *doubt*. When they find a new person, they cry out, "Yes! This is my magic person who can fill all my needs and give me happiness." Their fantasies and expectations about this special person have very little to do with who that person really is. Their focus is on what they need and what that other person can do to meet those needs.[51] A person such as this lives with the myth of the ultimate passion. For the person being pursued initially it may be flattering but in time suffocating. Does this fit anyone you know?

For people to fit the pattern of the obsessive lover, they need to meet four criteria. This includes having a consuming, intense, even painful preoccupation for a real or wished-for person in their life. They seem to be consumed by either possessing this person or being possessed by them. Here is where rationality breaks down. The person they desire must be unavailable to them in some way or may actually reject them. They may have said, "I'm not interested," "I'm not available," or "Get lost!" But it doesn't matter to the obsessive lover. The rejection actually feeds and frightens the obsessive love. Because of the unavailability or rejection, they begin to behave in self-defeating ways.[52] Their fear of rejection can have the same effect as having been rejected. And it's a self-defeating way to live life and create a healthy relationship. The rejections are creatively rationalized. Statements like the following are common:

> "I know that she dates other men, but they really aren't significant to her. She really cares only for me. She'll realize that soon."

> "I call him several times a day and he hangs up. He just can't face how much he cares for me. I guess he's overwhelmed by it and can't handle it. Someday he will."

> "He hasn't called for two weeks. It's happened before when work gets really busy. When it lets up, he'll be back."

But all these statements deny the truth.

When sex is a part of this kind of relationship, it further clutters the relationship. In most obsessive relationships, sex plays a major part. And it's usually very intense and pleasurable. The problem is it's used to measure the intensity of love, of compatibility, whether the other person cares, and leads to idealization of the other person. The obsessive person uses the sexual relationship as a sign of certainty that this relationship is "the one" for his or her life. But often the intense, passionate sex has been mistaken for love, and the short-term passion makes any rejection hurt even more.

As I have worked with couples in premarital counseling, I've found that about half of them have a pure sexual relationship. They are not having, nor have they had, sexual intercourse. For those who are engaging in sexual relations, I ask them to bring this to a halt and to maintain a pure sexual relationship until the wedding night. They agree to this, and in time some of them make a decision not to marry. Why? Several have said, including men, that now that there was no sex, they could see their problems more realistically and the driving passion that had seemed to be the glue that kept them together.

An individual can overcome an obsessive love difficulty. If you or someone you are seeing has this problem, put all involvement and dating on hold until it is resolved. It can lead to obsessive pursuit, revenge, stalking, and even violence. Do you or someone you know fit this list? An obsession with love can have the following characteristics, and it only takes a few of these to indicate a problem:

> —They yearn for a person who isn't physically or emotionally available to them.

> —They live for the time when their desired will be available to them.

—They believe that if they want them enough, eventually they will have to love them.

—They believe that if they continue pursuing this person long enough and hard enough, they will accept them.

—When they are rejected, they want the person even more, and continued rejections lead to depression or rage.

—They feel victimized because of the lack of response on the part of their partner.

—They believe only this one person can fulfill their life.

— They are so preoccupied with the person that their work is affected, their eating, sleeping, etc., or they call the person constantly and at inappropriate times, watch them, check up on them, etc.[53]

This may sound sick to you. It is. But it is reversible; the person can develop normal and healthy relationships.

Considerations for a Long-Term Relationship

If you are looking for a long-term relationship that will be fulfilling to both of you, there is no time limit on how much time to take to get to know this other person in all kinds of settings and under all sorts of circumstances. Work with them for two or three days straight on a mission project of your church or doing the cooking and cleaning up on a weekend for junior high students. Be with them on extended occasions with their family or close friends. If possible, spend a day with them at work, paint a room together, shop with them for several hours (groan!), etc.

How much time should you give to move from short-term to long-term? Let's say three months to a year. You can't rush this process, nor can you bypass it. I see and hear about couples all the time who execute a courtship bypass, but in most cases the surgery isn't successful and eventually the patient (the marriage) dies. Recently I heard about a couple who met and in seven weeks were engaged. Both said that it just "feels right." They haven't had time for any difference or crisis yet. Another couple in their twenties became engaged three months after meeting because of her dream of getting married, their physical relationship, and the extra money he would make by being married while in the army.[8]

There has to be time for the infatuation, physical attraction, chemistry, or whatever you want to call it to subside so you can deal with the real issues of life and allow love to develop. Whatever the initial chemistry was will hopefully continue and balance out, but much more needs to be added. If the relationship experienced intense passion because of sex and the romantic high begins to wane, couples who feel that the romantic high is essential usually do not stay together. The odds against eternal passionate love are insurmountable. When you understand this and choose to be satisfied with the quieter feelings of satisfaction and contentment, a relationship has more of a chance. Time lets this happen. Even secular sociologists and demographers have identified predictors of what contributes to a happy marriage and indicators of a marriage that lasts. Two of them are that you married after the age of 20 and you dated for a long time before getting married.[54] How have you been praying about this future step? Bringing a relationship before God and asking Him for clarity, insight, and wisdom is a significant step. Looking at the relationship in light of Scripture is another way to discover God's will. With every relationship, focus on Proverbs 3:5,6: "Lean on, trust *and* be confident in the

Lord with all your heart *and* mind, and do not rely on your own insight *or* understanding. In all your ways know, recognize *and* acknowledge Him, and He will direct *and* make straight *and* plain your paths" (AMP). Then ask yourself, Will this relationship lead me (or us) to a stronger and fuller expression of reflecting the Word of God in my life or less? The answer to this may be all you need.

Before pursuing a long-term relationship, list the indications that this has been satisfying enough for you to pursue. Seeing it in writing brings greater clarity. When I work with premarital couples, they think this issue through very carefully and thoroughly and bring to their initial session a list of ten indicators as to why this is the time of their life to marry. I'd like to see this happen at the transition from a short- to long-term relationship and once again when a couple begins to entertain serious thoughts about marriage.

Here are some indications or reasons that others have shared with me for your consideration. A man in his forties shared the following:

> After my divorce (actually even before) I began a biblically-oriented study into the reasons for the failure of my marriage. I believe that process has paid off quite well in terms of my building a genuine Christian (i.e., *godly*) lifestyle and learning the basic commitment and maturity required for a Christian marriage. I've also dated rather extensively in the last five years and have gotten to know many women from all walks of life. In the process, I began to formulate a list of *required* and *desirable* characteristics I would need in a significant woman in my life, based upon 1) biblical mandates and principles and 2) my personal preferences, desires, needs, hopes, etc. For the first time in my life, I have an established criteria or

value system by which to evaluate a potential partner.

This man did find his partner. His personal growth and careful planning paid off.

A woman in her thirties shared the following:

> The time is right because for the first time the person is right. There were others with many fine qualities, too, but along with these Tony is the right person. One thing that is so comforting is that when he has an "off" day and is disagreeable, grumpy, or is out of sorts, I still love him. That in itself is reassuring.

What about it? Are you emotionally and spiritually where you want to be and ready for what it takes in a long-term and hopefully permanent relationship? Have you dealt with all of your concerns? Have you completed the evaluative steps that are necessary? This may be your time to move forward.

When you're thinking that marriage is in the future, take the next step and begin premarital or pre-engagement counseling. The opportunity to spend six to ten hours with a minister or counselor can assist you in identifying issues which you may have missed, will help you eliminate future surprises, and will assist you in developing skills that you will need in marriage. Appendix B will give you additional information concerning the structure and resources of premarital counseling.

"How Do I Know If I'm in Love?"

A couple is sitting in my office for their initial session of premarital counseling. They've come with a mixture of expectations and apprehension, since they've heard the sessions will be very thorough. About halfway through our time together, I ask the man to describe in detail the love he has for his fiancée. After his response, I ask her a question which throws her, since she assumed her question would be the same. The question is, "How do you know that you love him? What convinced you?" Sometimes the responses are complete and full of substance, whereas others are lacking. I've heard remarks like, "Well, I just know that I love him or her. It can't really be explained." But perhaps it does need to be examined, explained, and even expanded. I've had individuals ask, "How do I know if I'm in love? How can you be sure? And what is love?" All of these are important questions.

One of my favorite cartoons depicts two chickens looking at two swans with necks intertwined and eyes glazed. In answer to the question, "What is love?" one chicken responds with, "Love is a feeling you feel when you have a feeling you've never felt before." That may be love, or it could be some bad onions you ate for lunch.

How would you describe love? How would you define it? What's the difference between love and infatuation? Is romantic or passionate love necessary in a relationship? And the big question, "How do you know when you're really in love?"

Let's consider a few basic facts about love:

1. *Love at first sight is rare.* An infatuated attraction may happen immediately, but true love needs time to develop.

2. *Love is NOT consistent.* Your emotional response to your spouse will vary over the months, years, and decades of a relationship.

3. *Most individuals can fall in love many times.* But the often involuntary physical and emotional attraction of "falling in love" should not be confused with the willful and abiding commitment to love selflessly the person who has captured your heart.

4. *The quality of courtship love will change and deepen in marriage.* And each succeeding level of love can be as exciting, rewarding, and fulfilling as the last.

5. *Love in a marriage relationship can diminish and even die.* Love must be carefully nurtured and cherished over the years if it is to endure the stress of two imperfect people living together.

I also like what M. Scott Peck says in his book *The Road Less Traveled* about the illusion that erodes so many marriages today:

> To serve effectively as it does to trap us into marriage, the experience of falling in love probably must have as one of its characteristics the illusion that the experience will last forever. . . . The myth of romantic love tells us, in effect, that for every young man in the world there is a young woman who was "meant for him," and vice versa. Moreover, the myth implies that there is only one man meant for a woman and only one woman for a man and this has been predetermined "in the stars." When we meet the person for whom we are intended, recognition comes through the fact that we fall in love. We have met the person for whom all the heavens intended us, and since the match is perfect, we will then be able to satisfy all of each other's needs forever and ever, and therefore live happily ever after in perfect union and harmony. Should it come to pass, however, that we do not satisfy or meet all of each other's needs and friction arises and we fall out of love, then it is clear that a dreadful mistake was made, we misread the stars, we did not hook up with our one and only perfect match, what we thought was love was not real or "true" love, and nothing can be done about the situation except to live unhappily ever after or get divorced.[56]

Love is not something that just happens; it must be cultivated so it can grow.

Romantic Love: Beliefs, Fallacies, and Benefits

Perhaps these thoughts are new to you or you're already aware of them. You may even be bothered by them, especially if you're a highly romantic person.

Romantic and passionate love are a necessary ingredient, but there must be more than this for a marriage to last.

Romantic love is a necessary part of the process, but it can also be the great deception in a relationship. But it makes us feel so good. Often the predecessor to romantic love is infatuation. Webster's dictionary defines this as "to make foolish, cause to lose sound judgment; to inspire with shallow love or affection."[57]

It's also been defined as foolish, all-absorbing passion, as well as *blind love*. You see what you want to see, but it's not really there. Or what you see is not what you're going to get! And when it dies, it's like stepping out of a plane without a parachute. The trip down is long and painful. Some biochemists believe that an amphetaminelike substance is released by the brain of an infatuated person and causes something similar to a drug-induced high. But when the infatuation stops, withdrawals occur. Psychologists suggest that most of the time infatuation involves falling for a person who fills some vacancy in your life, but your intended can't produce what you're after.[58]

Objectivity is low, and rose-colored glasses are in place. You see the other person as the answer to all of your problems and personal defects. The other person seems to fill in the missing parts of yourself. Life takes on a freshness and you see the other person as the best you can find. You feel omnipotent, and your attention and concern is for the other person. You may think this only happens to those in their teens, but I've seen it hit those in their twenties, thirties, and forties. Many people don't like to admit they are infatuated; rather, they say they have an intense romantic love for their partner. I looked up this word in the dictionary as well and found that *romance* or *romantic* means "an emotional calling; having no basis in fact: imaginary, visionary, marked by the imaginative or emotional appeal of the heroic, adventurous, remote, mysterious, or idealized; an emphasis on subjective emotional qualities; marked by or constituting passionate love."[59]

When there is romantic love, you feel that no one else has ever felt what you are feeling. Often there is an eerie sensation of "even though we've just met, I feel as though I've known you all my life." There seems to be an instant rapport or connection. But many say romantic love is a myth and a dangerous one for the marriage relationship.

As M. Scott Peck describes the "Myth of Romantic Love" in the passage just quoted:

> We have met the person for whom all the heavens intended us, and since the match is perfect, we will then be able to satisfy all of each other's needs forever and ever.[60]

There is an emotional high involved with romantic love. There are elevated feelings of delight, triumph, and the belief that "I can do now what I couldn't do before." Often it overrules the rest of the pain and disillusionment of our life and gives us a false promise that it will last forever. It thrives on uncertainty and novelty. Romantic love also acts as an anesthetic or a Novocain to the hurts in our life. This can occur whether there is sexual involvement or not. If sex is involved, the physical passion often creates an intensity to the romantic feelings that can only be maintained by peak sexual experiences. On the other hand, this intense love can cause couples to override their Christian values and have full sexual expression become the end result of their romantic experience.

But romantic euphoria will fade. That is a fact. M. Scott Peck also says,

The experience of falling in love is invariably temporary. No matter whom we fall in love with, we sooner or later fall out of love if the relationship continues long enough. This is not to say that we invariably cease loving the person with whom we fell in love. But it is to say that the feeling of ecstatic lovingness that characterized the experience of falling in love always passes. The honeymoon always ends. The bloom of romance always fades.[61]

Many people base their romantic love on physical attraction and soon end up making love physically. And within this intensity of passion they decide to marry. When this love diminishes, a new and more mature love needs to develop and replace it. But if it doesn't, the couple will probably divorce or have affairs. Either option is their attempt to recapture the feelings that have been lost. Physical attraction by itself, without the other elements of deeper love, will carry a marriage for about three to five years. That is all. Some of those three to five years may have been used up before the couple marries.[62]

If a couple marries with the romantic attraction stage as their basis, they can expect the romance to carry them for perhaps five to eight years before things begin to come unraveled and the criticisms and attacks on one another intensify.

What are the problems with a relationship just based on romance? Consider these beliefs and the actual facts about them.

Belief number one says, "Love is an overwhelming feeling that just comes over us." This is a false belief about love. Love is not something that just happens. Love is not all emotion, a rush of feeling that is totally and entirely uncontrollable. But when there is a powerful chemistry and you "just click," enhanced by romantic settings, experiences, and sexual encounters, you believe it does just happen. But believe it or not, this is not love. Romance and genuine love are not one and the same. Romance is like a hand grenade with the pin pulled out and a delayed fuse with an undisclosed amount of time remaining on it. Given enough time, it will go off.

Romantic feelings are not something you can choose or not choose to experience. It will probably happen to you. Just don't equate it with love.

A second belief is that having romantic feelings will always lead to happy endings, after all, "What could ever go wrong when we have such intense feelings?" Rational explanations to couples in this state rarely register because their rationality toward themselves has been turned off.

Sometimes one partner is aware their love object has deficits or isn't the best for them, but their love overrides good sense. But the worst possible basis for making a decision to marry someone is to do it based just upon romantic feelings. After all, if there is nothing else available, what will you hang onto when (not *if*, but *when*) these feelings pass? Years ago a woman that I know socially called, very excited to tell me that she had just gotten engaged and wanted premarital counseling. She said she had fallen deeply in love with this man she had known for six weeks and they knew they were meant for each other. "Isn't this wonderful?" she said. I shocked her by saying, "No, it's not," and proceeded to tell her why. She was offended, married the man, and divorced him two years later after discovering that he was gay. This could have been prevented.

A third belief is that our romantic feelings and the guaranteed outcome happen "because my partner is the perfect person for me." We see no flaws. Instead we overlook them or discount their existence. It's wonderful to find someone so good. But there is no perfect person.

Date someone long enough, and then you'll know. This is why long-term, extensive dating and knowledge of a person is the best preparation for a marriage that lasts. This involves working with the person on projects, seeing them under stress, and spending extensive periods of time with them and their family.

A last belief about romantic love is that it is totally spontaneous and just happens. This leads us to believe that loving someone is easy. Love is work. It is commitment. It is an act of the will. What is easy is romance, but not love. I like what Thomas Jones says about love and romance: "Romance is based on sexual attraction, the enjoyment of affection and imagination. Love is based on decisions, promises, and commitments."[63]

Is there any good that can come out of romantic love? Yes, definitely. Neil Warren in his excellent book *Finding the Love of Your Life* suggests,

> Passionate love performs a powerful service as long as it lasts. It focuses the total attention of two people on each other long enough for them to build an enduring structure for their relationship. The passion to love experience will never hold the two of them together forever. But building "enduring structures" for a relationship takes a lot of time and effort, and if two people are not attracted to one another physically, the hard work might never get done. That's another function of passionate love—the life-changing experience of being accepted and valued. When two people find themselves totally engrossed in each other, they often experience a dramatic boost in their self-esteem. For in the process of discovering that someone else finds them attractive, they begin to see themselves as attractive, too. Passionate love focuses a bright, positive light on each of the persons involved, and

both of them fall in love not only with each other, but also with themselves.[64]

You do need some natural physical attraction or emotional response. It's difficult to build a strong marriage if you don't feel a physical attraction to each other. I've seen people try to talk themselves into being attracted to another person. I can remember in college trying to talk myself into being attracted to a girl I took out once, but it was an exercise in futility. It either happens or it doesn't, and to say attraction is not important is a bit unrealistic. Dr. Neil Warren's words sum up the positive nature very well:

> I think God's invention of passionate love is one of the most magnificent parts of His creation. I am convinced that every person should have the opportunity to enjoy this kind of love at some time. There is no substitute for the deep-down love that two people have for one another. But in the early phases of a relationship, great care must be given to the expression of these feelings. Passionate love has a way of shorting out the brain and squashing rational thought. If conscious control is not exerted, the euphoric couple will begin to behave in a way that is damaging to the relationship and each individual.[65]

Premature sexual involvement is a negative for many reasons. One important reason is that it may fool the couple into marriage, because of what they are experiencing. Making a decision to marry at this stage without allowing the relationship to fully develop is like allowing a first-year medical student to perform brain surgery before completing schooling and hospital residency! You don't want to make a lifetime decision based upon just romantic or passionate love. Keep in mind that the greater the physical involvement, the more you tend to isolate yourself from your friends. The greater the physical involvement, the less you communicate. Physical involvement short-circuits growth.

What type of love should a couple move toward? *Phileo* is one kind, and this is friendship love. Whereas romantic love cannot sustain a relationship, companionate or friendship love can. If friendship has not yet been developed in a relationship, marriage is premature. A friend is someone you like to be with. You enjoy their company, you like their personality, you can play and work together. There are shared interests between the two of you. It's not that you are loved only because of what you share, but by sharing you develop a different kind of love. It means companionship, communication, and cooperation. One writer describes companionate love:

> This may be defined as a strong bond, including a tender attachment, enjoyment of the other's company and friendship. It is not characterized by wild passion and constant excitement, although these feelings may be experienced from time to time. The main difference between passionate and companionate love is that the former thrives on deprivation, frustration, a high arousal level, and absence. The latter thrives on contact and requires time to develop and mature.[66]

I have seen numerous marriages over the years fall apart because not only was this type of love nonexistent, but the couples also weren't even sure how to develop it. The greater the amount of time a couple can give to a relationship outside of the typical dating process, the more this kind of love can flourish. When *phileo* or companionate love has developed, couples will have this to stabilize their relationship when the romantic love fades. Unfortunately, some people with certain personality proclivities are almost addicted to the "high" or "excitement" of romantic love. When it diminishes, they fall apart or bail out to seek a new, exciting relationship.

Friendship Love

What does friendship love entail? It's an unselfish dedication to your partner's happiness. It's when the fulfillment of their needs becomes one of your needs. It's learning to enjoy what they enjoy, not just to convince them you're the right person, but to *develop* the enjoyment yourself as you share the enjoyment together. My wife genuinely developed a liking for trout fishing to the extent that she has her own set of waders and a float tube. I have genuinely learned to enjoy art and fine paintings. We both learned, and it brought us closer together. Friendship means you do some things together, but you're also comfortable with having your own individual interests, and you encourage each other in these. There is a balance between togetherness and separateness.

Friendship involves a certain level of intimacy in which there is an openness, a vulnerability, and an emotional connection. You also share goals, plans, and dreams, and work together.[67]

Agape Love

Another form of interpersonal love, *agape* love, can increase our gratitude as well as our constant awareness and remembrance of God's agape love for us. An attitude of thankfulness for all of life develops. We are able to see and concentrate upon the positive qualities and attributes of our spouse, which we might overlook or take for granted. Our mind-set and attitudes can be refocused because of the presence of agape love. An attitude of appreciation causes us to respond with even more love toward our spouse.

Agape love manifests itself through several characteristics. First of all, *it is an unconditional love.* It is not based upon your spouse's performance, but upon your need to share this act of love with your spouse. If you don't, your spouse may live with the fear that you will limit your love if he or she does not meet your expectations.

Sometimes you have to learn to love your partner unconditionally. Here is what one husband said:

> When I married my wife, we both were insecure and she did everything she could to try to please me. I didn't realize how dominating and uncaring I was toward her. My actions in our early marriage caused her to withdraw even more. I wanted her to be self-assured, to hold her head high, and her shoulders back. I wanted her to wear her hair long and be perfect at all times. I wanted her to be feminine and sensual.
>
> The more I wanted her to change, the more withdrawn and insecure she felt. I was causing her to be the opposite of what I wanted her to be. I began to realize the demands I was putting on her, not so much by words, but by body language.
>
> By God's grace I learned that I must love the woman I married, not the woman of my fantasies. I made a commitment to love Susan for who she was—who God created her to be.

Agape love is given in spite of how the other person behaves. This form of real love is an unconditional commitment to an imperfect person. And it will require more of you than you ever realized. But that's what you will commit yourself to when you marry.

Agape *love is also a transparent love.* It is strong enough to allow your partner to get close to you and inside you. Transparency involves honesty, truth, and sharing positive and negative feelings. Paul Tournier shared the story of a woman whose mother gave her this advice: "Don't tell your husband everything: to maintain her prestige and keep her husband's love, a woman must retain a certain mystery for him." Tournier commented, "What a mistake! It fails to recognize the meaning of marriage and the meaning of love. Transparency is the law of marriage and the couple must strive for it untiringly at the cost of confessions which are always new and sometimes very hard."[68]

Agape *love has a deep reservoir to draw from.* No matter what occurs, the love is felt and provides stability during times of stress and conflict.

Agape *kindness is servant power.* Kindness is love's willingness to enhance the life of another. It is the readiness to move close to another and allow him/her to move close to you. Agape is trying to be content with those things that don't live up to your expectations.

Agape love must be at the heart of a marriage. It's a self-giving love that keeps on going even when the other person is unlovable. This love will keep the other types of love alive. It involves kindness, being sympathetic, thoughtful, and sensitive to the needs of your loved one, even when you feel the person doesn't deserve it.

If you're in a relationship with someone now, consider these questions: Can you be happy with this person if he or she never changes? Are you loving the person you have now or an imaginary dream? And can you be happy with this person if he or she changes in ways you never dreamed of? A love with its roots in commitment will last through the pressures and pain of life's disappointments.

Think about this:

> Love means to commit yourself without guarantee, to give yourself completely in the hope that your love will produce love in the loved person. Love is an act of faith, and whoever is of little faith is also of little love. The perfect love would be one that gives all and expects nothing. It would, of course, be willing and delighted to take anything it was offered, the more the better. But it would ask for nothing. For if one expects nothing and asks nothing, he can never be deceived or disappointed. It is only when love demands that it brings on pain.[69]

Since agape love is the heart of the marital love relationship, let's think some more about this gift of love.

Agape love is a healing force. To demonstrate the power of this love, let's apply it to a critical area that affects marriage: irritability. Irritability is a barrier, and it keeps other people at a distance if they know it is present within us. It is the launching pad for attack, lashing out, anger, sharp words, resentment, and refusal of others' offers to love us.

Agape love is unique in that it causes us to seek to meet the needs of our mate rather than demanding that our own needs be reciprocated. Our irritability and frustration diminish because we are seeking to fulfill another person rather than pursuing and demanding our own need satisfaction.

Let's think together one more time about your love. Since it is sometimes difficult to really determine if what you are feeling is genuine love, there are several tests for love. In his book *I Married You*, Walter Trobisch has suggested five of them.

1. *The Sharing Test.* Are you able to share together? Do you want to make your partner happy, or do you want to become happy?

2. *The Strength Test.* Does your love give you new strength and fill you with creative energy? Or does it take away your strength and energy?

3. *The Respect Test.* Do you really have respect for each other? Are you proud of your partner?

4. *The Habit Test.* Do you only love each other, or do you also like each other and accept each other with your habits and shortcomings?

5. *The Time Test.* "Never get married until you have summered and wintered with your partner." Has your love summered and wintered? Have you known each other long enough to know each other well?[70]

Here are four additional tests from another author:

6. *The Separation Test.* Do you feel an unusual joy while in the company of each other? Is there pain in separation?

7. *The Giving Test.* Love and marriage are giving, not getting. Are you in love to give? Are you capable of self-giving? Is this quality of self-giving constantly evident?

8. *The Growth Test.* Is your love dynamic in its growth? Is it progressively maturing? Are the characteristics of Christian love developing?

9. *The Sex Test.* Is there a mutual enjoyment of each other without the constant need of physical expression? If you can't be together without petting, you don't have the maturity and love essential for marriage.[71]

Let's go back to one of the questions I mentioned at the beginning of the chapter: "Why do you love your fiancé?" Consider these reasons one man listed:

Reasons Why I Love Joan

1. Because her educational standards are high. I am of the realization that these standards will be instilled within our children.

2. Because Joan perceives life with such profound insights. She appreciates God's creation.

3. Because Joan makes a conscious and earnest effort to please others, even before herself.

4. Because Joan is able to meet my physical, spiritual and emotional needs. Physical, in that she is able to give warmth and comfort; spiritual, in that she is able to add biblical insights into everyday situations; emotional, in that she is able to be empathetic toward my sensitivities.

5. Because I have the freedom to share my most inward feelings, knowing that I will not be met with rejection, but rather, knowing that Joan will make an earnest effort to understand.

6. Because she values me. She appreciates my warmth and understanding. She appreciates my efforts to comfort and console her. I love being appreciated.

7. Because Joan has learned, and is continually learning, the art of submission without the threat of subserviency.

8. Because Joan accepts me for who I am, knowing my imperfections, and just as importantly, she is able to constructively work with me to my betterment.

9. Because I really enjoy her company. I enjoy walking and talking with her. We can talk about anything and everything.

10. Because she is open to growth and willing to change.

11. Because of her high moral standard, which will have a positive influence on our relationship.

12. Because of her extreme honesty.

13. Because I wish to give of myself to Joan. To be understanding, gentle, warm, empathetic—being able to listen with an open heart and arms.

Perhaps after all you've read about love in this chapter you wonder, "Is real love possible? How do I know if what I'm experiencing now is love?" Yes, it's possible, and hopefully this book will assist you in clarifying your future with another person.

We have all been called to be people of love. Love is actually a commandment from God. Again and again in Scripture, Jesus calls us to love. "Jesus replied, 'Love the Lord your God with all your soul and with all your heart and with all your mind.' This is the first and greatest commandment. And the second is like it: 'Love your neighbor as yourself.' All the Law and the Prophets hang on these two commandments" (Matthew 22:37-39 NIV).

Because love is a commandment, there are three conclusions that can be drawn from it:[72]

Loving others is a moral requirement. It is our responsibility to love even if others don't love us. In a relationship our emphasis then is to put our efforts on learning to love that other person rather than figuring out how to get them to love us.

Love is also an act of the will. We choose to love in our heart and mind. Love means choosing what is right and best to do rather than what I may want or feel like doing. It is this choice that will keep many marriages alive.

Love is not determined by our feelings. Nowhere in Scripture does it say to love others if you feel like it. We can't command our feelings. They come and go. They're like the tide in the ocean; they come in and then recede. Don't allow your feelings to be your guide. I've had a few people say, "My feelings of love for that person are gone." The shock on their face is evident when I say, "Great." Now they can learn true love, if they haven't already.

Definitions of Love

Our society and the media have given us a false portrayal of love. Scripture gives us a valid portrayal. As you continue to consider the love that is necessary for a marriage, reflect on these thoughts given by people who were asked to give their definition of a loving relationship:

> "A loving relationship is a choice partnership. Loving someone in which even imperfection is seen as possibility and, therefore, a thing of beauty; where discovery, struggle and acceptance are the basis of continued growth and wonderment."

> "A loving relationship is one in which individuals trust each other enough to become vulnerable, secure that the other person won't take advantage. It neither exploits nor takes the other for granted. It involves *much* communication, much sharing, and much tenderness."

> "A loving relationship is one in which one can be open and honest with another without the fear of being judged. It's being secure in the knowledge

that you are each other's best friend and no matter what happens you will stand by one another."

"A loving relationship is one which offers comfort in the silent presence of another with whom you know, through words or body language, you share mutual trust, honesty, admiration, devotion, and that special thrill of happiness simply being together."

"A loving relationship is an undemanding exchange of affection and concern, rooted in total honesty and continuing communication without exploitation."

"A loving relationship is one in which the loved one is free to be himself—to laugh with me, but never at me; to cry with me, but never because of me; to love life, to love himself, to love being loved. Such a relationship is based upon freedom and can never grow in a jealous heart."

"A loving relationship is one in which each one sees the beloved not as an extension of self but as a unique, forever becoming, beautiful individual— a situation in which the persons can bring their own special I to each other, a blending of selves without the fear of loss of self."[73]

Counterfeit Love Styles

ou're sick! Sick! Sick! Sick! You think you love me, but what you call love is smothering me. I don't need this and neither do you. I want a healthy relationship, not this slop!"

They sat in my office, one pleading and the other attacking. Their marriage wasn't working out, even though they both claimed they loved each other. I've seen so many couples like this over the years, some dating and others married. Something was wrong with their relationship. The so-called "love" they said they had for each other was expressed in a strange manner. It was contaminated. It is amazing how we can take something so pure and pollute it. Oftentimes love is a disguise. There are several forms of counterfeit love.

The Pleaser

Unfortunately, some people equate being a pleaser with love. There are men and women in relationships who constantly give and give and give, but it is not because of love. It is either because of guilt or because some of their own needs are being met. They need to give to others in order to feel good about themselves. It is like being hooked on helping, and they become help-aholics. A pleaser is a person who is dominated and guided by their emotions. They do the right things for the wrong reasons. They do loving things rather than being a loving person.

Dr. Les Parrott describes the counterfeit styles of love so well in his book *Love's Unseen Enemy.* Each style has several characteristics.

Pleasers have this overwhelming need to please. It is as though they live to make people happy. As you watch them, they appear to be conscientious and caring. They go out of their way to make others feel comfortable. They're especially good at remembering to do the little things others overlook. They're so approachable and agreeable, and when asked to do something they usually do more than you request, even with a warm smile. But these acts of love aren't voluntary—they're driven. They feel personally responsible for the happiness of others. If their partner is unhappy, they feel guilty. They're driven to do too much. Because of this they easily attract others, but in a relationship they may end up feeling used. Most pleasers tend to be women.

Pleasers are the givers of life. Not only do they avoid receiving, but when they do receive they feel uneasy. They feel guilty and begin thinking of ways to repay. Pleasers also have a performance mentality. They must do things right away, and they want to look good. They need approval in order to keep their guilt in control. They live for the applause. They live with a fear of failure, and unfortunately, this can drive them to comply with unrealistic requests for their help. Saying "no" to anyone is unheard of, because they view that as a personal failure. This is not a healthy, biblical way to love another person.

Pleasers have a sense of responsibility that is way out of proportion. If married, they believe they're responsible for their spouse's well-being and happiness. It reminds me of a rescuer, a self-appointed lifeguard. But the ones they tend to rescue aren't drowning.

To them, self-denial is not a means to an end, but an end in and of itself. But it makes loving behavior no longer loving. They turn into a martyr and, in the process, may drive people away. This in turn pushes their guilt and they try harder, which pushes others away even more.

Pleasers are some of the great conflict avoiders of the world. They defer, give in, say "yes" when "no" is more appropriate, and allow wrong to continue. It's not surprising many pleasers that I've seen in premarital counseling have violated their own values as well as Scripture by engaging in premarital sex. But they do have limits. If pushed or cornered into conflict, they either give in and blame themselves or erupt like a volcano, because they're so unskilled in resolving conflicts.

Have you ever tried to get a straight answer or a personal preference from a pleaser? Don't. They defer decisions and avoid giving their own opinions. They don't want to choose and decide. Otherwise the decision they make may not please you.

In a marriage relationship a pleaser lives for their partner's affection. They look for it and hold on to any small measure. But... they also expect their partner to know what they want or need without ever telling them. Can you even imagine a pleaser expressing what they need to their partner? Not really! Any withdrawal or diminishing of intimacy on the part of their partner is a disaster. And time after time I have seen the same scenario played out in my office. The pleasing spouse sits there and says, "I just don't understand it. I love him so much, and I tried to please . . . yet it seems that the more I try to please the more I seem to push him away from me." It's true. Their partner felt smothered and constricted.

A husband married to a pleaser said, "It makes me sick. I wish she had more backbone and would stand up to me. Let's have some conflict. I'm tired of having a 'yes' person for a spouse." Pleasers tend to create some of the very problems they wish to avoid. What about you? Does any of this sound familiar? If you're dating someone who fits this profile, just remember: The love you think is there is counterfeit.

If these characteristics fit you, let's take it a step further. Your involvement with others could even be more intense than a pleaser's. There may be another term for it. Here is a way to clarify if your love and helping responses are genuine. Evaluate your caring thoughts, feelings, and actions using the following statements. For each statement rate yourself from 1 to 10, with 1 signifying that the statement definitely *does not* reflect you, 10 signifying that it definitely *does* reflect you, and 5 being somewhere in the middle. For any statements you rate above 5, consider the reason for reflecting this characteristic. If these do not reflect you, who do they pertain to that you know?

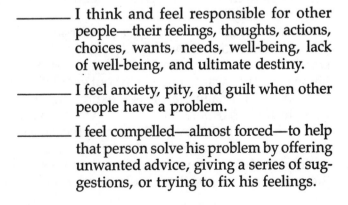

_____ I think and feel responsible for other people—their feelings, thoughts, actions, choices, wants, needs, well-being, lack of well-being, and ultimate destiny.

_____ I feel anxiety, pity, and guilt when other people have a problem.

_____ I feel compelled—almost forced—to help that person solve his problem by offering unwanted advice, giving a series of suggestions, or trying to fix his feelings.

_____ I feel angry when my help isn't effective.

_____ I anticipate other people's needs.

_____ I wonder why others don't anticipate needs.

_____ I find myself saying "yes" when I mean "no," doing things I don't really want to do, doing more than my share of the work, and doing things other people are capable of doing for themselves.

_____ I often don't know what I want or need. When I do know, I tell myself that what I want or need is unimportant.

_____ I try to please others instead of myself.

_____ I find it easier to feel and express anger for injustices done to others than for injustices done to me.

_____ I feel safest when I'm giving.

_____ I feel insecure and guilty when somebody gives something to me.

_____ I feel sad because I spend my whole life giving to others and nobody gives to me.

_____ I find myself attracted to needy people.

_____ I find needy people attracted to me.

_____ I feel bored, empty, and worthless when I don't have a crisis in my life, a problem to solve, or someone to help.

_____ I abandon my routine in order to respond to someone in trouble or do something for someone else.

_____ I overcommit myself.

_____ I feel harried and pressured.

_____ I believe deep inside that other people are responsible for me.

_____ I blame others for the spot I am in.

_____ I believe that other people make me feel the way I do.

_____ I believe other people are making me crazy.

_____ I feel angry, victimized, unappreciated, and used.

_____ I find other people become impatient or angry with me for all the preceding characteristics.

If you tend to respond to these statements with a 6 or above, you may be what is called a codependent. Not all pleasers fit the pattern of a true codependent, but they may be close to it. Your life reflects the negative traits of the pleaser. Two resources to help you are *When Helping You Is Hurting Me* (Harper and Row) by Carmen Renee Berry and *Love's Unseen Enemy* (Zondervan) by Dr. Les Parrott III.

You may feel like challenging this profile of a pleaser. Others have. I've heard it from both husbands and wives: "I thought one of the elements of marriage was to put the other person first, to meet their needs and to please them. Aren't we to be a servant to one another?" Definitely yes, but in a healthy, loving way, not for the reasons given previously.

Let's consider the concept of servanthood as an expression of love in marriage. In marriage we are called to be a servant to one another.

Do not merely look out for your own personal interests, but also for the interests of others. Have this attitude in yourselves which was also in Christ Jesus, who, although He existed in the form of God, did not regard equality with God a thing to be grasped, but emptied Himself, taking the form of a bond-servant, and being made in the likeness of men. And being found in appearance as a man, He humbled Himself by becoming obedient to the point of death, even death on a cross. Therefore also God highly exalted Him, and bestowed on Him the name which is above every name (Philippians 2:4-9).

Jesus voluntarily submitted to becoming a "bond-servant," looking out for our interests rather than His own. In the same way, the apostle Paul tells us to "be subject to one another in the fear of Christ" (Ephesians 5:21).

Notice one important point: We must never *demand* that our partner be our servant or live up to the clear teachings of Scripture. If we feel that we have to demand it, or even to mention it, then we become more concerned with meeting our own needs than with being a servant.

Servanthood is the identifying mark of every true Christian believer.

To put it simply, a servant's role is to make sure that the other person's needs are met. In a husband-wife relationship, being a servant is an act of love, a gift to the other person to make his/her life fuller. It is not something to be demanded. It is an act of strength and not of weakness. It is a positive action which has been chosen to show your love to each other. Hence, the apostle also said, "Be subject to one another," not limiting the role of servanthood to the wife.

A servant may also be called an *enabler*. The word *enable* means "to make better." As an enabler we are to make life easier for our spouse instead of placing restrictive demands upon him/her. An enabler does not make more work for the partner, nor does he/she hinder the other from becoming all he/she has been designed to become.

A servant is also one who *edifies* or builds up the other person. The English word *edify* is derived from the Latin word *aeds* meaning "hearth" or "fireplace." The hearth was the center of activity in ancient times. It was the only place of warmth and light in the home, and the place where the daily bread was prepared. It was also the place where people were drawn together.

Edifying is often used in the New Testament to refer to building up another person. Three examples of edifying are expressed in the verses below: 1) personal encouragement, 2) inner strengthening, and 3) the establishment of peace and harmony between individuals.

> So let us then definitely aim for and eagerly pursue what makes for harmony and for mutual upbuilding (edification and development) of one another (Romans 14:19 AMP).

> Let each one of us make it a practice to please (make happy) his neighbor for his good and for his true welfare, to edify him—that is, to strengthen him and build him up spiritually (Romans 15:2 AMP).

> Therefore encourage (admonish, exhort) one another and edify—strengthen and build up—one another (1 Thessalonians 5:11 AMP).

Look back at the characteristics of a pleaser and at the reasons for them responding in this way. Do they fit with this expression of love? Not really. Love is to be genuine. A genuine person is able to express his or her own self and feelings in appropriate ways, rather than suppressing them or masking them.

> When you always put up a false front before others, you may start to confuse your true identity with the "character" you are portraying. You may begin to wonder, *"Who am I really?"* That's one of the delights of being a Christian. We can accept who we are because of the way God sees us through His Son Jesus Christ.
>
> A main ingredient in genuineness is sincerity. When someone is sincere, you can relax in the comfort and security that he or she is trustworthy. Sincerity also is a biblical quality. Paul prayed that the love of the Philippian believers would "abound still more and more in real knowledge and all discernment, so that you may approve the things that are excellent, in order to be sincere and blameless until the day of Christ" (Philippians 1:9-10, NASB).
>
> Our word *sincere* comes from a Latin word which means "without wax." In ancient times, fine, expensive porcelain pottery often developed tiny cracks when it was fired in the kiln. Dishonest merchants would smear pearly white wax over the cracks until they disappeared, then claim the pottery was unblemished. But when the pottery was held up to the sun, the light would reveal the cracks filled in with wax. So honest merchants marked their porcelain with the words *sine cera*— without wax. That's what is meant by genuine sincerity: no hidden cracks, no ulterior motives, no hidden agendas.[74]

Being genuine with others involves another risky ingredient: transparency. Transparency, the ability to be seen for who you really are, is a rare commodity these days. It's easier and safer to wear a mask than to let others see who you are inside. But it's hard to build a relationship with someone wearing a mask. Jesus encouraged transparency when He said, "Blessed are the pure in heart, for they shall see God" (Matthew 5:8. The word *pure* literally means "clean, uncontaminated, sincere, without corruption, alloy, or guile and honest in motive." I enjoyed reading Chuck Swindoll's illustration of transparency:

> Last night I decided to try something I had never done before to drive home a point. At my last birthday my sister gave me a full-face rubber mask . . . one of those crazy things that slip over your entire head. She told me she'd give me ten dollars if I'd wear it into the pulpit one Sunday (my kids raised it to fifteen dollars), but I just couldn't do it! Well, last night I wore that ugly beast when I got up to speak. I figured if anybody could handle it, this gang could. *It was wild!*
>
> I didn't call attention to it. Without any explanation, I just stood up and began to speak on being authentic. There I stood pressing on, making one statement after another as the place came apart at the seams. Why? Anybody knows why! My mask canceled out everything I had to say, especially on *that* subject. It's impossible to be very convincing while you wear a mask.
>
> I finally pulled the thing off and the place settled down almost immediately. As soon as it did, everybody got the point. It's a funny thing, when we wear *literal* masks, nobody is fooled. But how easy it is to wear invisible ones and fake people out by the hundreds week after week. Did you know that the word *hypocrite* comes from the ancient

Greek plays? An actor would place a large, grinning mask in front of his face and quote his comedy lines as the audience would roar with laughter. He would then slip backstage and grab a frowning, sad, oversized mask and come back quoting tragic lines as the audience would moan and weep. Guess what he was called. A *hipocritos*, one who wears a mask.

Servants who are "pure in heart" have peeled off their masks. And God places a special blessing on their lives.[75]

Transparent people are remembered, appreciated, and trusted. Genuine people are not pleasers. Transparent people are not pleasers.

Why am I discussing styles of loving? It's simple. Before you become too attached in a relationship, you want to be able to identify the warning signs either of your own or your partner's pattern of counterfeit love.

The Controller

A controller pattern, in many ways, is the opposite of a pleaser. Yet they both have a strong need for acceptance. But they certainly try to get it in different ways. A pleaser yields power to others in their desire to be loved, but a controller takes over and takes charge to gain the respect of others. A pleaser has an overabundance of sympathy but very little objectivity. The controller, being just the opposite, has a great amount of objectivity but doesn't know the first thing about sympathy. Controllers are very analytical. Even though this helps them understand the needs of others, the purpose is usually to gain control over them. Controllers can usually be identified by seven characteristics of how they relate to others.

Their need to be in control is obvious, and they use two means to accomplish this. Fear expressed through intimidation is typical, and they are very adept at discovering and using weaknesses in other people. The other tool is quiet, and it can be activated in the spouse of a controller by a word, rolling of the eyes, or a gesture. Any mistake is noticed and used to guide the erring spouse into line with their agenda.

Controllers are very self-reliant, and in marriage teamwork for them is not a possibility. Totally independent, they create their own vacuum of loneliness, for their style of independence alienates them from other people.

The absence of emotion in their life helps to create a marriage in which their partner ends up starving for closeness and intimacy. The emotional bonding which is necessary for a healthy relationship fails to happen. Many controllers have never allowed themselves the opportunity to feel. If they do, they keep it in. I see numerous people who have only learned to cry on the inside. Many controllers only feel anger. Joy, delight, and sadness are missing from their lives. They think about emotions but rarely feel them. When their spouse expresses emotions, they're probably quite uncomfortable with the display and quickly try to deal with them rationally.

When it comes to expressing loving behaviors that are genuine, controllers are quite inept. What you may see as graciousness, politeness, kindness, or even being very sociable has a purpose in mind—to take control of the other person. Having love as an end result has no real meaning, but using love as a means to an end makes sense to them. If there is an interest in another person, it's for a purpose. Their partner, married or unmarried, ends up feeling used. But many controllers believe they are loving their partner. Using them is an expression of their love.

Rules, rules, and more rules is their way of life. And the more rigid they are, the better. There is a right way to do things—it's their way, and it's the only way. They know what's best for others and will orchestrate their life. If you're in a relationship with a controller, you'll find yourself being forced to conform in one way or another. Not all, but many controllers have the additional problem of being a perfectionist. This will make your life even more unbearable. (For detailed assistance in learning how to handle and change a perfectionist or controller, see chapter 11 of *How to Change Your Spouse Without Ruining Your Marriage* by Gary Oliver and this author, Servant Publications.)

Controllers are people who live by labels which includes name-calling. The most common one I see in counseling is when the controller (often the man) tells his wife, "Now you're not going to go and get all emotional on me again. You know we can never resolve anything when you get that way. When you pull yourself together, then perhaps we can continue."

Their style of communication has one characteristic: demanding in words, intent, and tone. They're bottom-line people who cut right to the heart of a matter.

There is one last factor for you to consider when a relationship contains a controller. It is very difficult in a marriage for intimacy to develop when one partner is overly dominant or controlling and the other is submissive. A controller won't open up and reveal his or her inner life and feelings for fear of losing the position of power or control. And the submissive partner is fearful of being open and vulnerable, because he or she could be attacked and overwhelmed by the other person. In a new book, *When Love Dies*, the results of the research indicate that one of the main reasons for individuals losing their love for their partner and eventually divorcing is a lack of mutuality in the marriage. Mutuality is a respect for one's partner which is based on the belief that each person is an equal in the relationship. When acts of mutuality are missing from a relationship, love dies. Lack of mutuality includes controlling or dominating a partner or disregarding their beliefs, opinions, desires, etc., or forcing them to do something against their will. It's showing disregard for who they are.[76]

Now, have we talked about anyone you know—a former partner, a current one, yourself perhaps? Let's keep in mind that the majority of pleasers are women and the majority of controllers are men. Often they attract one another as they strive to fill the empty places in their personalities. In a marriage to a controller, you end up feeling misunderstood and dominated. Controllers don't take the time to foster and nurture a close relationship. They get their own needs met, and any guilt or shame which might break through to the surface is repressed by activating the guilt of their partner.[77]

If you are dating someone who fits this profile and you continue the relationship, ask yourself, "What is the need in me that causes me to be drawn to this kind of person? What am I hoping they will do for me?" Reflect on what your marriage relationship would be like five or ten years from now. Are you prepared for emptiness in your marriage?

The Withholder

There is yet one other style of relating. This person, a witholder, lives in a self-made castle of protection. Close relationships which involve empathy or sympathy are nonexistent. A withholder lives with the fear of rejection, usually because of some deep past hurt. He or she is a survivor, but one who has been so damaged they don't know how to relate effectively. They have a deep sense of shame, and many of them protect themselves by avoiding close relationships. They don't carry much hope for a healthy relationship.

I have seen a number of withholders over the years in counseling, and usually it is their partner who patiently and persistently pursued in order for the relationship to develop in the first place. (But too often the relationship is carried by one partner, even though that partner hopes the other will learn to respond.) But all too often the pursuing person becomes weary of doing all the work and wants out. Many withholders are what I call "blame collectors." They personalize problems and believe that whatever happens is because of something they've done wrong. Their entire focus is upon themselves. For this reason they are unable to relate effectively with others. Aside from guilt, their emotional life is flat or nonexistent. It's like looking at a monitor of a person's heart and seeing not the spikes of each heartbeat but a flat line. A withholder has put so much time and energy into avoiding pain and has done such a good job, he has deadened the other emotions as well, such as hope, joy, and love.

There are several characteristics that are important to identify. You need an awareness of these in case this is a description of you or someone you may be interested in pursuing. Withholders are pursued by those who believe they can bring them out of this shell.

A withholder has a need to withhold his or her inner wounds. Their suffering is not as obvious as that of a pleaser, nor do they strive to control. They may look very well put together. But they are living with an attitude of resignation. They feel that nothing good will ever happen to them. Why dream when dreams are shattered? Why get your hopes up just to be disappointed? Many withholders avoid close relationships because safety comes from being distant. I've seen some men like this who were pursued by women who believed, "But he has so much potential. If he'd just let God get a hold of him, he could be the man he's supposed to be. I can make that happen for him." And in their desire to remake, refashion, and change him, they marry and are usually miserable, because it doesn't work. There are some partners, though, who marry a withholder and let them be the way they are. But that's not much of a marriage either.

Keep in mind that the withholder's focus is on themselves. It won't be on you. If you choose a person like this, you won't be the one their eyes are upon. Socially, many of them don't relate very well. They're too involved in taking their own emotional temperature and protecting themselves.

Withholders have a sense of helplessness and believe nothing they do will make any difference or improve their lot in life. Along with this they are overcautious in their relationships. If someone shows an interest in them, they doubt that it's sincere. They think that the other person has a hidden agenda and wants something from them. They feel that trusting the sincerity of other people is a foolish step because you end up getting burned.

A characteristic of withholders which is the source of major problems that I have seen in marriages over the years is passive aggressiveness. This is an indirect, underground, subtle but definite resistance. It is such a concern that it's the subject of entire books, including *Living With the Passive-Aggressive Man* by Scott Wetzler. It's a very frustrating pattern to have to deal with. It destroys relationships that would otherwise make it. There are many forms of passive-aggressive behavior. Procrastinating is a favorite choice. Procrastinators put off responsibilities or delay doing something for someone else. If they're an hour late to pick you up, *you* end up feeling responsible, because they say, "Are you sure you said 10:00? I was sure you said 11:00. Oh well." And after hearing this a couple of times, you begin to doubt what you said.

Forgetting is another favorite way to display resistance, because it can be turned back on the other person:

"Are you *sure* you asked me?" or "Are you *sure* that was the time we agreed upon?" They may use your car and leave it messy and with an empty tank. They use a check and fail to write it in the checkbook. You may be talking to them about something important and they either leave the room, get up and turn on a noisy blender, fix a drink, or increase the volume on the TV.

It seems as though withholders are a bit masochistic, because they seem to gain something from being hurt. Perhaps they feel good about themselves for suffering silently and they resent the person whom they perceive as having hurt them. This is all the excuse they need to hurt back by withholding their lives. If their partner is hurting, don't expect much from them. They don't know how to empathize, because of their fixation on their own pain. They are grudge collectors. Each hurt is kept and transformed into resentment which just fuels the withdrawal pattern.

One of the most painful and frustrating characteristics is the way they communicate. They don't overpower, but rather defect or are totally noncommittal. They won't invest an opinion or make a decision. They evade, use silence, and leave the room. They have a number of simple sounds which speak volumes, such as sighs and groans, and the sounds of silence. You ask, "What's wrong?" and the reply is "Nothing" or "You should know," or a shrug as they leave the room. Sometimes withholders make poor choices in marriage partners because they are afraid to select the right one for fear they'll be abandoned. They have a negative perspective and negative expectations in their relationships. You could be a very positive, loving partner 95 percent of the time, but this will be ignored, because the 5 percent is what the withholder fixates upon.

If you tend to be a withholder, before you consider a relationship seek out a professional counselor. Your life can be different if you're willing to give it a chance. Two books for your reading are *Love's Unseen Enemy* by Dr. Les Parrott III (Zondervan) and *Your Tomorrows Can Be Different Than Your Yesterdays* by this author (Revell).

If you are dating such a person, ask yourself, "Why?" What are your hopes and dreams for them after you marry? Ask the person to seek counseling before you invest any more time in this relationship.[78]

After becoming aware of three problem styles in a relationship, perhaps you're wondering if anyone is or can be healthy. Definitely yes. There are healthy, mature individuals in all stages of growth. We are called to be constantly growing in all phases of our life. Paul said, "Now your attitudes and thoughts must all be constantly changing for the better" (Ephesians 4:23 TLB).

The Lover

Dr. Parrott discusses a fourth and healthy style of relating which he calls "The Lover." This is a person who is capable of reflecting the agape love discussed in the previous chapter. This is a relatively guilt-free person. This is how he describes a lover.

You may be a **Lover** if...

—you listen for the unspoken feelings behind a person's message.

—you objectively assess a situation before jumping to conclusions.

—you realize you cannot make everyone happy.

—you enjoy receiving from others without feeling indebted.

—you are not obsessed with what others think of you.

—you put yourself in others' shoes.

—you are aware of your own needs but are also sensitive to others.

—you do not use blame or intimidation to get your own way.

—you deal with conflict openly and maturely.[79]

Can you give examples of how you reflect each of these characteristics? If you're in a relationship at the present time, are these the traits you see in your partner and what they see in you?

For a person to be like this, they need a solid sense of security and identity in Jesus Christ. They know who they are and feel good about themselves. In a marriage this person can accept the uniqueness of their partner, can learn from them, be open and vulnerable, communicate their needs openly and honestly, and above all else empathize.[80] Do you really understand what it means to empathize?

Empathy comes from the German word *einfulung*, which means "to feel into" or "to feel with." Empathy is viewing life through another's eyes, feeling as another feels, hearing the story through the perceptions of the other person. All Christians are called to empathy by bearing one another's burdens (Galatians 6:2) and by rejoicing with others in their joys and weeping with others in their pain (Romans 12:15).

Some people confuse empathy with apathy and sympathy, which sound similar but actually are quite different. Sympathy means you are overinvolved in the emotions of others. Sympathy can actually undermine your emotional strength so that you are incapable of helping when you are most needed. Apathy means you are uninvolved with others. Empathy means walking with another person in his inner world.

Apathy has *no* feelings for another—which is what controllers do; sympathy is feeling *for* another—which is what pleasers do; and empathy is feeling *with* another. Apathy says, "I don't care"; sympathy says, "Oh, you poor thing"; and empathy says, "It looks like you're having a difficult time today."

Empathy means a person sees their partner's joys, perceives what underlies those joys, and communicates this understanding. When someone has empathy for us, we experience the satisfaction of being understood and accepted because another person sees our point of view. That's the kind of satisfaction we can give to other people as we express empathy to them.

What do you want in your relationship? Now that you are aware of the possibilities, it's your choice.

When You're Dating the Wrong Person— How to Get Out of a Relationship

group of eight single men and women were sitting at a table in a restaurant. They seemed to be having some kind of a celebration. But there was something different about it. They were all there to celebrate the end of a relationship. Each had been involved in a dating relationship without a future. Every man and woman in the group had found the courage to take that decisive step of calling it quits, and they were ready to move on in their lives. Listen to some of their stories.

Linda: "I don't know why I hung on so long. I knew the second month of the relationship that it wasn't going to work. Oh, I know I'm a fixer. I thought I could fix Ted, but how can you fix something when they don't even know that something's broken? It just seemed to go on and on. He seemed content, but I sure wasn't. I wished I'd pulled the plug earlier. Maybe I was just comfortable having someone around.

Ted was better than nothing, but it's when I realized that nothing was better than Ted that I was motivated to do something. Now I can move on with my life."

Phil: "Breaking off a relationship is no picnic. I think I hurt as much as she must. That's what kept me connected to her for so long. I didn't want to hurt her. I tried several times, but I couldn't stand it when she cried. I felt so rotten. We both knew there were too many obstacles, but we kept trying. She loved me so much. She told me I'd never find a woman who would love me as much as she did. She's probably right, but I didn't want to spend the rest of my life with her. I didn't love her. At least not in the same way she loved me. It just wouldn't work. It's been two weeks now and my sense of relief is now stronger than my hurt."

Tina: "The longer we went together, the more he moved into my life. He was nice and kind at first, but then he became so possessive. He wanted to dominate all the time. I couldn't go anywhere without Bill wanting to be there. He gave me so much and seemed to adore me. But his possessiveness scared me. He didn't want me involved with my friends anymore and they're all turned off toward him. He started checking up on me and asking me where I've been, who I've talked to, who's called on the phone. He tells me things that scare me, too, like, 'I can't live without you,' and 'You're my whole life and source of existence.' I was always wondering what he would do if I broke up. Well, I've found out. I had to tell him in person, over the phone, send letters, but he wouldn't listen. He'd ignore whatever I said and come back with 'You don't mean it. You're just upset, right?' And that really made me mad. I won't even talk to him now or even acknowledge him when he comes around. I hate to be rude, but what do you do when they don't believe you? I feel like I'm being stalked by Bill. He's out of my life as far as the relationship goes, but he's still interfering with my life."

Reasons for Hanging On

You've probably been there—involved in a relationship that is dead and you're looking for a parachute so you can bail out and escape. But along with relief, breaking up brings with it a whole jumble of other feelings as well. I don't think it's ever easy to break up a relationship, even when it's the best step for you. It takes two people to make a relationship work, and you might think it takes just one to break it off. But it doesn't. It takes both. The other person has to accept the fact that it is over, or they can make your life miserable. Many people struggle with this decision. One of the major dilemmas singles make is not knowing when and how to say "no" to a relationship. When the possibilities for dating someone else are slim, you may feel an additional pressure to stay in a relationship. The person may not be that wonderful, but it sure beats being alone.

What keeps you from ending a relationship that you don't want or isn't healthy for you? Often you get hooked into the other person's feelings. Most of us don't want to cause another person pain. Even if breaking up is the healthiest decision for both of you, your partner will be hurt. If they are very sensitive or dependent, it will be more intense. If they tend to be an obsessive lover, it will be even worse. They will hang on like Superglue and pursue you in a multitude of ways.

Another reason for the struggle over breaking up is the power of sexual pleasures when you've been involved in this way. You know it's best to sever the relationship, but your mind wanders back to the times of intense pleasure and you begin to listen to your hormones. And sometimes it overwhelms your best intentions. You say, "Well, just one more time." And each time can intensify your guilt as well. If your partner is highly seductive and discovers they can use this to keep you trapped, you will be controlled in more ways than you realize. And if sex is part of your relationships, you might stay with the person who is safe rather than run the risk of struggling to find a new relationship in which a sexually transmitted disease might be in the offing, including AIDS.

You may stay in a poor relationship because you're addicted to security. As bad as a relationship might be, people feel safer staying in a relationship they know something about rather than risking one that's unknown and scary.

The tension or ambivalence that a person feels when attempting to break off a relationship can be very intense for some. A 30-year-old woman described the combination roller coaster/bumper car ride she felt she was on as she struggled through the termination of a relationship:

> I thought I was going a bit crazy myself. My feelings were in turmoil. One minute I seemed to delight in Terry, but then I felt controlled and oppressed by him. One minute I loved him, but the next I resented him and what he did. Oh, he was attentive, that's for sure, but he didn't know when to stop. I felt invaded by him like an intruding army. And now, when I try to break it off, I feel guilty. What's wrong with me?

It almost sounded like she wanted in and out of the relationship at the same time, and that will confuse anyone. Sometimes you can be addicted to a person even when you want him or her out of your life. There is such a need filled by a person that anyone will do.

Many women hang onto unhealthy relationships. They're hoping that somehow the man will magically change and become Prince Charming. But as one radio personality said, "When you kiss a toad, they don't turn into a prince—you just get slime in your mouth."

Think of it in this way: If you're struggling to get out of a relationship, but remaining, you are more concerned with getting your short-term needs met than your long-range goals such as marriage. The longer you put off the inevitable, the more you shortchange yourself. You are hurting yourself more than the other person.

Gene shared with me another reason many people hesitate in breaking up:

> Norm, I know what I want in a relationship. I thought it through carefully and I have my list, but I'm just not sure I'll be able to find what I want. I've got to compromise, I guess, but it is very uncomfortable. Some days I feel it's best to get out and then I think "I'll never find her anyway," so I just make do.

Making do doesn't last a lifetime.

I see a number of singles staying in a relationship because they think they're in love. The kind of love they are experiencing, however, is coming from defeats from the past or because of mistaking a physical entanglement for love.

Some people live their life on the phrase, "But I love him . . . " or "But I love her . . . ." Basing a decision for life on fickle, misleading feelings is one way to keep yourself in pain. I've heard both men and women say, "I just love that person. Oh, I know they're . . . , but . . ." The words

I've heard them use to describe their partner ranged anywhere from *cold, angry, raging,* and *controlling* to *uncommunicative, distant, abusive,* and *violent.* The descriptive statement is made and followed up with the words, "But I love him or her." Remember, the words "I love him/her" don't erase the descriptive words that were used before. In fact, aside from a radical upheaval in that person's life, or some intense therapy, there won't be any erasure of that description.[81]

Jim Smoke in his ministry to the divorced describes the dilemma this way:

> Sometimes you've been in a relationship for such a long time you struggle with wanting to break up vs. look at all the time and effort we've put into this. Perhaps we can overcome these difficulties. Or you may be getting pressure from your family and friends. They keep saying, "Come on. How long is it going to take? You know you're right for one another. You've just got the typical jitters that anyone has. Go on, tie the knot." And you begin to think, "Well, if they think we're right for each other, maybe there's something that I'm missing." But pressure like this you don't need. You must be certain. Letting someone else make a decision for you won't work since they don't have to live with the decision, you do.[82]

He then goes on to describe several different ways people attempt to rescue others, which leads to immense struggles in attempting to break up a relationship so it doesn't lead to marriage.

Years ago I was working with a couple in premarital counseling who had been going together for five years, but it wasn't working out because of numerous differences and problems. I finally suggested that they put the relationship and pending marriage on hold and work on their own individual issues. The response I heard was, "Finally someone has given us permission *not* to marry. We've been getting all this pressure from everyone to go ahead and 'tie the knot.'" The sigh of relief I heard from them is a sigh that many experience when they make this decision. Over a period of time, families of the couple may have developed a close friendship and socialize together. The breakup then is not just of the couple, but could be of the friendship. And that, too, can create undue pressure upon the couple.

Emotional and Financial Rescue

Emotional rescue involves you in trying to make the other person's pain go away. You hear another person's painful story of a broken relationship or tragic divorce and you jump in feet first to rescue them. But too often the intensity of their leaning on you in their state of vulnerability is overwhelming. Or then again, some people enjoy having others lean all over them. But it only leads to a sick relationship.

A relationship rescuer finds a new person before they're ready for each other. They have to have a relationship, regardless of who it is. I see many of these couples simply living together. Each has a need for a person and a body. They know it's not going anywhere, but they have the comforts of home. Often they don't think of breaking it off unless they've got their eye on someone else so they can avoid the empty transition time.

I've seen single mothers become enmeshed in a relationship because they are being rescued financially by the men in their lives. Divorced mothers have a difficult time with their reduced standard of living. It's hard to resist financial aid, but usually there are strings attached. How do you break off a relationship when you know you'll lose several hundred dollars of support each month? And yet this is no one with whom you would want to spend the rest of your life![83]

When Is a Relationship Over?

If you're ambivalent about your relationship or struggling with trying to break it off, perhaps it would help to make a list of the eight to ten consequences of staying with the person. Perhaps seeing the consequences on paper will jar you into action. At the same time, make a list of what you are getting from this relationship that is 1) healthy for you, 2) improving your Christian walk and testimony, and 3) causing you to go downhill anyway. Is this the best for you, or could you do better? Where is God's will in all of this? What is He saying to you? Here are some other questions to consider:

1. What is your partner not being or doing that you want?

2. How long have you been thinking about ending the relationship?

3. What would have to happen for you to feel this might work out?

4. How often have you brought up the issues and concerns to your partner? What has happened since then?

5. Are you in a situation in which your partner is willing to do anything, but that doesn't matter to you anymore?

6. What does this person do for you when you're with him or her?

7. Does their attitude and behavior toward you increase your positive feelings about yourself?

8. Do you feel more attractive being with them?

9. Do they encourage your strengths or elaborate on your weaknesses?

10. Are you a better person by being with them? Is the other person trustworthy?

11. Do you constantly make excuses for them? Do you or the other person constantly try to change one another?

12. Is your relationship with Jesus Christ enhanced by being with them?

A woman shared with me, "It's so hard because I don't hate him. He really is a nice person, but he's just not for me. It would be so much easier if he were a rat and I could despise him, but I don't!" You don't have to hate or even dislike a person in order to break up. If the relationship isn't beneficial for you, then it's not for the other person, regardless of what they say. Did you ever think about that? You can also end a relationship when you care about the other person, but you know it just won't work for the two of you. Even if you give your partner a list of eight things to change and they do all eight, it's being done for you. Unless they want to change because they see the value, what makes you think the changes will last? I've heard people say, "If the relationship was meant to be over, then I wouldn't doubt my decision, would I? I seem to waiver back and forth, back and forth." This is normal. Don't let that stop you.

A relationship is over and needs to be cut off when . . .

1. You want out more than you want in. This doesn't have to be a mutual decision.

2. Both of you want out and you don't want to work on the issues. Sometimes a couple will say, "We'll still see each other though as 'friends'

since we enjoy each other's company." Why? That's just keeping you from investing time and energy in recovering and then finding someone who could be your life partner.

Perhaps the reason you want out of the relationship is that it seems unfair to you. Your partner may have changed their expectations for you or they may be threatened by you for some reason and try to sabotage your efforts to grow and develop. You could be the one contributing more to the relationship than your partner, but he or she seems satisfied with their level of giving. Do you threaten your partner in some way, or are you threatened by them for some reason? These signs are danger signals.

Perhaps you feel you are giving too much. But is your partner asking you to give in that way or are you choosing to do it for some reason? Sometimes the other person is self-centered or a taker, or it could be you are giving in order to prove your love and desirability or to hang onto their love. And that could be one of the reasons that you have difficulty breaking off the relationship.

Breaking Off an Engagement

Perhaps one of the most difficult relationships to break off is an engagement. It's as though when you became engaged you've made a public announcement to the world, "I'm going to marry this person. They're so wonderful. I'm thrilled." Then, what does it say when you become unengaged? "I made a mistake. They're not wonderful. Something is drastically wrong. I don't love him/her. They don't love me." Perhaps that is what keeps some people from taking this step. So instead, they end up in a difficult marriage or even a divorce.

But as painful as a broken engagement is, it is nowhere as devastating as a divorce can be. Over the years I've heard many people say, "I knew during the first year that I'd made a mistake," or "It was the second week of the honeymoon that I knew I should have listened to those warning signals inside of my head." Perhaps the most drastic one came from a young man who was divorcing his wife. He said he knew as soon as he married her that he had made a mistake. And when asked, "How soon did you know?" he said, "When I saw her walking down the aisle." How tragic!

Unfortunately, many people still believe that an engagement has the same level of commitment that a marriage is supposed to have. It doesn't. Approximately 40 to 50 percent of engagements in our country break up. Over the past five years, of all the couples that I have seen in premarital counseling, 30 to 35 percent decided *not* to marry, and some at the last minute. In all but two of the cases, the couple made the decision themselves without my having to recommend this step. A friend of mine shared with me that 80 percent of the couples he works with in premarital counseling make a decision not to marry. Over the years I've seen couples who have canceled the wedding just a week or two prior to the wedding.

One woman in her twenties realized that she didn't fully love the quality young man to whom she was engaged. She had hoped that after being married she would fall in love with him. Two weeks prior to the wedding, which would have been a very large and elaborate service and reception, she told her father, "Dad, I have some bad news for you. I'm sorry, because it's going to cost you a lot of money for nothing, but I just don't love my fiancé. It would be wrong to go through with this wedding." Her father responded, "Honey, don't be concerned about the money. I'm more concerned about you and your happiness. Whatever you feel is best, I'll back you." And the wedding was canceled. Two years later she met the man who was to become her husband. Her act took courage. It was disappointing and painful to many people, but some of the wisest decisions of life are.

You can expect even more pressure from other people when you break an engagement than when you break a long-term relationship. You might wish you could go into seclusion to escape the embarrassment and all of the questions or even genuine offers of concern. But whenever any relationship is broken, whether it be long-term or an engagement, it may be better to take charge of it by making a statement. This will help put yourself and everyone else at ease. One of the best ways I've seen this happen is by formulating a letter to give to the significant people in your life (friends and relatives), stating what has happened, how it's impacted you, and the best way for them to respond to you. People have been doing this for years when they experience a breakup, the death of a close loved one, a divorce, or even having a disabled person in the family. A letter could read like this:

Dear _____,

Because you are a significant person in my life, I wanted to share with you a recent event in my life that will probably affect me for some time. As you know, _____ and I have been dating exclusively for the past three years. It appeared to us and to many others that we were on our way to marriage, but that doesn't seem to be the case. I (or we, depending upon the situation) have decided that it would be best after all this time to dissolve our relationship and each of us move on with our lives. There are reasons for this and after much thought, discussion, and prayer, I/we feel this is the best step to take. I'm sorry for the disappointment this may cause you as well as any feelings of awkwardness you experience, since many of you are friends of both _____ and me. For some of you, this will mean a loss of doing things with us as a couple as we have done in the past. So it will take some adjustment on your part, as it will on ours.

You may be wondering how to respond to me at this time and what to talk about and what not to say. Actually, you could feel free to respond to me as you have in the past. I can handle references about _____ and me. It's not something you have to avoid. For a while, I may avoid going to some of the places that _____ and I frequented while I adjust to my new status. I probably won't go into any more detail about this decision, but suffice it to say it is the best for me at this time in my life. Thank you for your support and your prayers.

A letter such as this is genuine, and it appears there is not too much trauma associated with the breakup. If it was traumatic, it would be helpful to mention that it was devastating and that you will cry and be upset from time to time. Let them know specifically what you need from them, and share the fact that you may be recovering for several months. Usually other people have a timetable for our recovery that is unrealistic, and their expectations need to be altered. There will still be very close friends and relatives that you will talk with and go into greater detail with. But not everyone needs this, and many people who are curious and/or concerned will be helped by your letter. It also protects you from having to share the situation several times a day. The recounting of it again and again can become exhausting and painful.

The Best Time to Break Off a Relationship

When is it best to break off a relationship? As soon as you know it's not going to work out. You need to listen to your heart, your thoughts, and the Lord's guidance. You need to trust yourself. Parts of the relationship may be positive, but are these strong enough to carry the rest of it? I've known some who know after the initial phone conversation, initial meeting, three months, or three years later. Once you know, then the time you wait is wasted since it delays your recovery, and thus your development of a new relationship. You will waiver back and forth and experience confusion. That's normal. There may be a relationship in which none of that occurs, and you know absolutely that this one is over and out! That, too, can be normal. Watch out for the immobilizing statements you may make that will keep you trapped. They include:

"I just hate hurting another person."

"What will everyone think?"

"What if they're really angry with me? I can't handle that."

"I don't know what to say or how to do it."

"It's just too difficult."

Every time you make such a statement, you begin to believe it even more, and it becomes more difficult to take that necessary step.

How to Break Off a Relationship

Now the big question: "How do you break off a relationship?" How do you say "no"? Consider the following suggestions:

1. Decide whether you want to do this in person, over the phone, or in a letter. And whatever you do, if you are serious about not seeing this person again, don't be vague or give double messages or leave the door open. So if your decision comes during a first date or you keep running into the person at work, face-to-face may be the best. If it's long-term, sometimes the letter may be easier for you since the person can't immediately respond, has to think about it, and can't pressure you to change your mind. They will want and need to talk to you at some time, however. Whatever you do, don't let them hear it from someone else.

2. Be gracious and polite. You could share something positive at the same time you let them know you would prefer not going out with them again. Statements like, "Thank you, but I would rather not," work well. However, if you add the phrase "right now" or "at this time," they will think your resistance is just temporary and you'll be back. Don't say, "I'll get back to you" or "Call me later," if you want this fledgling or long-term relationship to be over.

But make it genuine. You may just want to say, "Thank you for the time you've invested, but I'm just not interested in pursuing the relationship any further." You don't have to give them a list of your reasons if they pressure you to know why you don't want to continue. Just use the broken-record technique and continue to repeat your statement word for word as you initially stated it. Especially in initial dates or short-term relationships, you are not obligated to give your reasons. All it does is give the other person control or power over you, and now they can begin to attack your reasons.

If it's been a long-term relationship, sharing the reasons may be helpful for personal growth. Be sure to say that your reasons are how you feel and it's from your perspective. Don't expect the other person to agree with you. They may become defensive and try to talk you out of your perspective as well as your decision. You may need to add that you do not want to argue the case or defend it, and you have already made your decision. Sometimes it helps to acknowledge their feelings and say that you could well understand they could be surprised, hurt, or angry. But keep in mind that no matter how they respond, they are responsible for it. Don't take the responsibility on yourself and carry a load of blame or try to make them feel better. If there are any items for you to return, it's best to do so at this time. If things need to be moved, do this as soon as possible.

If your partner has been untrustworthy to you, such as lying about who they are, their work or financial status, their Christian beliefs, or if they sexually harassed you, took and used money, or were unfaithful to you, they need to be confronted. I've seen too many situations in which the person was let off the hook with no confrontation. They were never exposed for what they were. They need to experience the natural consequences and discomfort of their sinful behavior, so either they experience conviction and come to genuine repentance or so others don't fall prey to their pattern of destructive behaviors.

I've seen cases in singles' fellowship groups in churches, because of a pattern of non-Christian behaviors such as misappropriation of the partners or resources, continual sexual misbehavior, or date rape that the offender has been asked to leave the group. And it doesn't take long for the word to spread as to the reasons. I've seen some cases where because of the volatile and unpredictable behavior on the part of the person on the receiving end of the breakup, a pastor or a couple of close friends were asked to be present when the person shared that the relationship was over. This was done for safety reasons.

Unfortunately, there are those who don't take "no" for an answer. They may have an obsession with you, be addicted to having a relationship, or are just so hurt and angry they may want to make life miserable for you. In any case, your safety, welfare, peace of mind, and future are at stake.

If you need to be very emphatic and assertive, plan in advance what you think you will need to say and practice making these statements out loud if you know this will be difficult for you. You cannot be subtle or appear uncertain, especially if the other person doesn't want to hear what you're saying or is resistant to the whole idea. Don't let the other person back you into a corner or get you in a defensive position. You could use statements like the following:

> "I understand this is upsetting, but our times together are over. This is not something I want to discuss, since it's not negotiable."

> If they persist in calling at home or work— "I'm going to hang up now. It won't help either of us to continue to talk, and if you call again I will hang up."

> "Please don't contact me in any way. It's just better that we go our separate ways."

> "What you're doing feels like harassment, and if you continue I will obtain a restraining order so we can both go on with our lives."

Sometimes the reluctant partner believes they know your thoughts and feelings better than you, so whatever you say may not register. The more information you give, the more you build their hope that you are not serious. *Remember that! It's true.* The more you explain, the more you encourage them to persist. Sometimes people have said, "It seems cruel to have to be this way or to break up like this." That's not true. This is fair and loving. What is cruel is hanging on and prolonging a "going-nowhere" relationship when you know it's over.

You may need to take some further steps to get the message through. This may include such drastic steps as screening all calls with an answering machine, changing your phone listing to an unlisted number, telling mutual friends to alert you if your former partner is coming to an activity, or suggesting that you not be asked to an event if the other person is coming.

TEN

"Are We Compatible?"

e've been dating for three years. We're not kids anymore—we're both 32. We seem to get along well most of the time, but I wonder... I wonder if we're really compatible or compatible enough to make a marriage work. What do you think?"

What Is Compatibility?

Good question. You may be taken back, though, by my answer. Compatibility isn't something that just happens—you make it happen. Couples who are dating think they are compatible, but they are not. You need the marriage relationship for the opportunity to learn to become compatible, and it takes the first decade of marriage for this to become a reality. You obtain this over a period of time.

Many people use the word *compatible*, but they don't fully understand its meaning. The dictionary defines it as "capable of living together harmoniously or getting along well together; in agreement, combine well, etc."[84] And the trend in the reason for divorce in our country is incompatibility.

To become compatible means you and your partner will be making some changes. You *can* change. You *will* change. In fact, you *must* change or you'll stagnate. And believe it or not, you will change your partner. It is possible, and it is all right to do so. Change is one of the ingredients of a healthy marriage. If you didn't change, it would imply that you're perfect and have no need to grow. And we both know the response to that belief!

Marriages which reflect compatible partners have an ingredient called mutual education. This means that both partners have become skilled teachers as well as receptive learners. Without this, a relationship could be in jeopardy.

Mutual education is a gentle process. It involves positive modeling of the desired attitudes or behaviors for your partner as well as the willingness to flex and change. It also involves gentle prodding, sensitive reminders, encouragement, believing your partner can change and succeed, and avoiding blaming and rebuking. It focuses on the positive. You want to manage that change so the end result is positive.[85]

If this is what is meant by compatible, what are the areas to be concerned about? What about physical attraction—is it there? Is it similar? I've talked with both men and women who have said they love the other person, but they're not really turned on physically by their partner. Everything about the relationship was going well, but the physical attraction was low. Perhaps the question is, What is it that you expect to happen physically? Could it be your expectation level is unrealistic?

Sometimes individuals compare their partner with a previous partner or their fantasies or even their responses when watching pornographic materials. Don't compare.

It will hinder your present relationship. It's difficult to compete with fantasies or memories anyway. Strong physical attraction and desire by itself will not sustain a marriage, as we have indicated elsewhere. I think there needs to be some mutual interest to the extent of wanting to fulfill your sexual needs with the other person. Mild sexual attraction and desire coupled with other areas of compatibility and friendship is a healthy response, because most of your time together in marriage is actually nonsexual.

People who fixate on and fantasize about having intense peak sexual encounters regularly when married often end up feeling, "Is that it?" They're let down. Also keep in mind that you will probably notice other attractive members of the opposite sex when you are engaged or married and be physically attracted to them. You can and will feel sexual desire for more than one person at a time. I like the thinking of one author who said,

> It is the nature of erotic desire that it can be invested in a variety of directions, a point that Paul seems to have well in mind in I Corinthians 7. When he advises Christians to marry "because there is so much immorality," his point is not, "Marry the person who attracts you so strongly that you can't think of anyone else," but "Because of the possibility of multiple attractions, determine to invest your sexual energies in one person, your spouse." This doesn't change the fact that I may be naturally inclined to be attracted to others, but it does underline the crucial need for commitment and determination not to let my interests stray outside of the marriage relationship.[86]

And keep in mind your physical desire, interest, and intensity will fluctuate after you are married. That, too, is normal.

Intellectual Compatibility

Since intimacy in several different dimensions is the bonding material which holds a marriage, it's important that we look at these for potential compatibility. Intellectual harmony or compatibility is another ingredient, but it doesn't mean you have to have the same degrees, number of degrees, vocational interest, etc. You probably won't see things the same or even think the same. Your learning styles may be different in that one may enjoy learning through what they see and the other through what they hear. Being married provides an opportunity for each of you to grow intellectually and also discover to a greater degree your spiritual giftedness.

Some who marry are avid readers, and some are not. I am the reader, but it's not Joyce's main source of learning. Sometimes this is affected by time availability as well as vocational pursuits and time of life. In the past few years, Joyce has had more time to pursue reading. She is one who verbalizes more about what she has learned than I do, and so we are learning together. We're open to being challenged by the other person's knowledge, insights, and opinions, which creates growth in both of us. Respecting your mate's abilities and differences is part of intellectual compatibility.

Communication Styles

But underlying this area and the others is the ability to communicate with one another. Your communication is the lifeblood of your relationship. When it's gone, so is your relationship. You may think that you're communicating well at this time. You may think you're connecting with your partner at this time, but are you really? For compatibility to unfold, each of you will essentially need to learn to speak one another's language. And the emphasis is upon learning to do so. The reason you probably aren't speaking the same language yet is because of gender differences, personality differences, and learning-style differences. All of these are reflected in your communication patterns.

When you marry, it's as though you marry a foreigner with their own culture, set of customs, and language. Because each of you is entering into a foreign culture, think about the two kinds of travelers who visit foreign countries—the colonizer and the immigrant. A colonizer wants to visit another country to experience it from his own perspective instead of from the inhabitants' point of view. Upon entering the country, he looks for signs in his own language and seeks out people who speak his language as well. He looks for the familiar and doesn't really venture into uncharted territory. Nor does he attempt to learn even the basics of the language. He is totally dependent upon the other people from his country who can guide him around and interpret for him. When he interacts with local residents, he doesn't get very far, even though he's been there for months. They're puzzled by what he says, and he can't comprehend them either. It's not a happy experience for either.

The other type of person is like an immigrant. He is somewhat of an adventurer. He actually prepares for the trip by orienting himself to this foreign culture. He reads books about the culture, the customs, the history, and the food of this new country and even attempts to learn everyday phrases of the language. In order to be able to converse better, he may even take a class in their language before he leaves. When he arrives at his destination, he is eager to discover all that he can. He searches out historical sites, tries all the new foods, reads as much as he can in the language of the country, and uses his newly formed verbal skills where possible. He may even enjoy living with a family of that country for a while in order to fully capture the flavor of this new world.

As the immigrant attempts to speak this new language, the people respond in a helpful manner. They help him pronounce strange words. Often, if they are at all adept in the traveler's language, they will begin to speak it to make him more comfortable. Thus, they perfect their own skills as well. They seem delighted that he has made an attempt to learn their language, and they can both laugh at some of his mispronunciations. The immigrant has an enjoyable time, whereas the colonizer ends up being frustrated. This illustration is just like a marriage relationship. Each person has a choice.

What does this mean in everyday practice? Take a close look at your personality characteristics and the way in which you communicate. Then do the same for your partner and compare the two. Where each of you is different from the other, make an effort to learn how to take those differences and balance them out. Then adapt your communication style to match your spouse's. Essentially you will be talking the way your partner does, and he/she will reflect back to you your own unique style of talking.

Speaking your spouse's language includes not only vocabulary but also the person's packaging. What do I mean by packaging? It refers to whether a person is an amplifier (sharing great volumes of descriptive detail) or a condenser (sharing little more than the bottom line). (I mentioned this briefly in the first chapter).

If your partner is an amplifier, go ahead and expand. If he or she is a condenser, keep it brief.

Amplifiers give a number of descriptive sentences as they talk, while condensers give one or two sentences. In approximately 70 percent of marriages, the man is the condenser and the woman is the amplifier. Neither is a negative trait, but the amplifier wishes his or her partner would share more, while the condenser wishes his or her partner would share less. It is only when each of you adapts to the style of your partner that compatibility begins to happen.

If your partner is an amplifier, give lots of information and detail. Keep it brief for condensers. You can always expand if the condenser wants more. But we also have to take into consideration someone's seeing, hearing, or feeling preference. This preference reflects how a person learns best and is a must in learning to connect or be in sync with one another.

There are other ways in which our communication style varies. These need to be altered so that it's easier to communicate with each other. Remember that in learning to become more flexible you are not denying who you are or squelching your personality. The flexibility you learn in discovering how to be compatible will assist you in other relationships in your life, including the business world.

Some individuals are very literal when they talk. They stick with the topic and answer what they've been asked. They don't speculate or rely on hunches. They tend to move from point 1 to 2 to 3 to 4 and conclude with 5. Sometimes when asked a question that needs a great deal of explaining, they respond in a format similar to a newspaper article. They give you a summation sentence, then some of the details, and finally they expand.

Others, though, are not literal when they talk. They go by hunches and love to speculate and consider all the possibilities. They may go off on detours as they explain something. They don't stick to the subject but instead go around the barn a few times. They may not finish a sentence before switching to another and then another. They tend to move from point 1 to 3 to 2 to 4 and then to 5. It makes perfect sense to them.

When asking a question or sharing a new thought, they give you the details first and then identify the topic.

Now, do these two styles sound familiar? You're probably one or the other, but not totally. You have both capabilities, but one is your preference or your strength. You can learn to use your nonpreference side more than you realize. In doing this you adapt to the other person in your life, who may be the opposite of you.

There is another example of how we can become more compatible, and it has to do with the way in which we learn. You may learn best through what you see or what you hear or through your feelings. Do you know what your preference is? Do you know your partner's? Each of you has a dominant sense through which you prefer to communicate and receive communication. But you need to become aware of these so you can adapt your communication style to your mate.

> A visual person relates to the world around him in terms of how things look to him. This is how the person learns best and 70 percent of people are visual. When he imagines he visualizes, and when he remembers, he recalls a picture. He experiences life through his eyes. He is primarily a watcher—movies, TV, sporting events, people, art exhibits or museums, scenery. He probably prefers reading, collecting items at which he enjoys looking, taking pictures, and looking at you. He is often concerned with how he looks to others. A visual person talks about how things look rather than how he feels. Often a visual person tends to withdraw and brood when upset rather than talking through the problem. Is this anyone you know?
>
> Visual people prefer face-to-face conversations over using the telephone and respond well to written messages.
>
> How can you tell if a person is visually oriented? Listen to the words that they use. Here is a list of statements that are more typical of a visual person:

From my point of view...

I see what you're driving at.

That looks like a sure thing.

That's really clear to me.

What you're picturing is...

I don't know; I've drawn a blank.

Show me what you're getting at.

There's a clear pattern to this.

It's beginning to dawn on me.

You could use the following in response to the visual person:

I'm beginning to see your point of view.

That looks good to me.

What you shared with me really lights up my day.

You know, I can just picture that.

I see what you mean.

Practice using visually-oriented words, especially if they are new to you. Write down a list of visual words—as many as possible—and look for ways to use them in conversation with your visually-oriented partner. If you usually say, "That feels good to me," change it to "That looks good to me" when you are talking with a visual person.

If you're going to marry a visual person you must adjust to their dominant style of perception. For example, if you are planning to buy new chairs for the family room, you will want to discuss with them how the room's appearance will improve in addition to how comfortable the chairs will be. If you want to escape to a quiet retreat with no phones and few people, emphasize to them the scenic aspects of the location.

... The auditory man or woman wants to hear about life. This is how this individual learns best and 20 percent of our population falls into the auditory category. This individual relates more to sounds than sights. Reading a book, the auditory person hears words silently rather than seeing pictures. You need to tell this person more than you show him or her. This individual prefers talking about something to looking at it. Long conversations are important to the auditory spouses and they tend to remember what they hear better than others. . . .

If you want to share feelings, the auditory person will best understand you if you verbalize how you feel. Auditory people hear equally what is said and not said, and they are astute at picking up tonal changes and voice inflections.

Auditory people fall into two different categories. Some feel compelled to fill the silent moments of life with sound: talking, playing the stereo, humming. But others prefer quiet. Why would an auditory person opt for silence? Because many of them are carrying on internal conversations, external sounds are an interruption. Sometimes a silent auditory person's intermittent spoken responses may not make sense to you because he fails to relate the ongoing conversation in his head.

Romancing an auditory partner must include saying, "I love you" again and again. But how you say it is as important as how often you say it. Discover the words, phrases, and tones that best convey your spoken love and use them often.

Here are some of the words and phrases an auditory person uses:

> That sounds good to me.

> Let's talk about this again.

> Boy, that's music to my ears!

> People seem to tune him out when he's talking.

> Harmony is important to me.

> I hear you clear as a bell.

> Tell me a little more about it.

> Give me a call so we can discuss the proposal.

> Your tone of voice is coming through loud and clear.

What kind of responses should you use with auditory people? The same type of words and phrases as they use. Instead of asking, "Would you like to go see that new movie with me?" ask "How does attending that new movie sound to you?"

You may say, "Changing the way we talk to one another sounds like a pointless game that requires a lot of work." Work, yes; game, no. Effective communication requires being sensitive to, and diligently accommodating, the uniqueness of your partner. By learning new ways to talk we climb out of our communication ruts and become more flexible. Changing your style of communication can make the difference between holding that person's attention and being ignored.

. . . Some people tend to be very feelings-oriented, although it is more often true of women than men.

(When it comes to learning, only 10 percent fall into this learning style even though many more are very feelings-oriented. Thus a visual person can still be very feeling.) Feelings-oriented people tend to touch a lot. They often desire to develop deep relationships.

Feelings-oriented people often show their feelings even though many of them do not verbalize them well. You can usually read happiness, sadness, anger, love, or delight on their faces or hear these emotions in the tone of their voices. And they are concerned about how others feel toward them. A feelings-oriented man who can effectively verbalize his emotions can be one of the easiest husbands with whom to live.

The feelings-oriented person often uses the following words and phrases:

> I have some good vibes about this.
>
> I have a sense about that.
>
> I like to get close to you.
>
> That person was so sensitive.
>
> I'm so happy today. Yesterday I was unhappy.
>
> I like being near you.

You will also hear words like *touch, tense, pressure, hurt, touchy, soft, smooth, handle,* and *relaxed* from a feelings person. Whereas the visual person says, "It looks good to me," and the auditory person says, "It sounds good to me," the feelings person will say, "It feels good to me," or "I'm comfortable with that," or "I understand how you feel."

If your partner is visual, don't demand that he/she open up and respond on a feelings level. First, he/

she has to connect with you on a visual level to feel comfortable. If your feelings are shared gradually, in a visual style, your partner will begin to relate to you. It's not always the easiest for a visual person to express his or her feelings in words.

Explain to your partner that you can see their feelings even if they're not expressing them. Ask how things look to them first rather than how they feel. In time you can ask, "How would you express that if you were to use my feelings words?" and he/she just may be able to do it.[87]

This is just an introduction to the process. I would encourage any person, no matter how old you are, to read chapters 4-9 of *How to Change Your Spouse (Without Ruining Your Marriage)* by Gary Oliver and this author (Servant Publications, 1994) and *TypeTalk* by Otto Kroeger and Janet M. Thuesen (Delecarte). (These resources can be ordered from Christian Marriage Enrichment, 1-800-875-7560.)

Emotional Compatibility

Emotional compatibility is such an important connection that if it isn't there or the potential isn't there, any of the following could occur if you marry:

1. You could end up as a pair of married singles existing separately.

2. You or your spouse could become emotionally starved and vulnerable to an affair.

3. You could end up getting a divorce.

I have seen all of the above happen, and sometimes all three within the same marriage. It's very sad. Perhaps the most vivid descriptive portrayal describing the depth of emptiness that can occur in such a marriage comes from the epitaph on a headstone in a cemetery in San Antonio, Texas. It was described by Max Lucado in his book *Six Hours One Friday*:

> Then I saw it. It was chiseled into a tombstone on the northern end of the cemetery. The stone marks the destination of the body of Grace Flewellen Smith. No date of birth is listed, no date of death. Just the names of her two husbands and this epitaph:
>
> > "Sleeps, but rests not.
> >
> > Loves, but was loved not.
> >
> > Tried to please, but pleased not.
> >
> > Died as she lived—alone."[88]

Many people have lived this way. I doubt if you want to. As I conduct premarital counseling, it is possible to predict in advance which couples are the ones in which emotional intimacy is nonexistent or the potential for its absence in marriage is evident. Some couples are shocked by this. I've seen couples work on emotional intimacy until it happens, while others postpone their wedding so they can reevaluate, and some break up.

Women tend to be more adept at sharing feelings and being in tune emotionally with their environment. They have a heightened sense of intuition. It's the way God created them. And society encourages and reinforces this tendency. Men have other strengths and have to work at this area of their life. Usually it doesn't occur naturally. Most men have been raised emotionally handicapped. We haven't had good role models to emulate, and we haven't been encouraged to be aware of our feelings nor develop a vocabulary to use in sharing them. But this problem can be corrected. It is possible for anyone to learn, if they so desire.

Perhaps nonemotional people will never match their feelings-oriented partner, but they can develop enough for them to become compatible emotionally. I encourage men to work through three resources before they marry. Two are books—*If Only He Knew* by Gary Smalley and *Real Men Have Feelings Too* by Gary Oliver. The other is a tape series by Stu Weber, *Tender Warrior*. The help offered in these resources has made a significant difference in many marriages.

Spiritual Compatibility

Even more important than the emotional is the spiritual dimension. For compatibility to occur, it takes more than both of you knowing and loving Jesus Christ as your Savior and Lord. Just because you may be compatible here doesn't mean that all your conflicts will go away. This is just one area. Being spiritually compatible isn't measured just by both of you belonging to the same church, liking to attend church three times a week, or having the same spiritual gifts. Your unique personalities come into play in terms of how your faith is experienced and expressed. There are many differences which do not negate compatibility.

From my perspective this is how I would view spiritual compatibility: Beliefs are vital. These would include each of you having a personal relationship with Jesus Christ which includes a desire to follow Him and a desire that others would come to know Him as well. The importance and value that each of you places on Scripture as the guide for your life is part of compatibility. But this still allows for diversity as well. One of you may be pre-tribulation in your theology and the other post-tribulation, but you respect each other's perspective in an area where there are differences. One of you may read the Scripture a half-hour a day and the other five minutes. One of you may listen to Christian radio all day and the other once in a while. These differences are not a measure of spiritual maturity or compatibility. Do you respect one another's spiritual uniqueness in each area, such as the type of Christian music you listen to, speakers you prefer, form of worship, etc.?

I believe that a core issue is the ability to communicate about your spiritual life with one another. Can you discuss Scripture *together* or engage in Bible studies? Do you *share* prayer requests, and pray together as well as for one another? Is there hesitation or resistance when you share spiritual thoughts, concerns, or beliefs? Do you each take the initiative to encourage one another to grow spiritually? Do you consider one another's spiritual gifts and encourage each other in strengthening and reflecting the meaning of spiritual compatibility? It's best to see this develop prior to marriage as one of the elements that draws you to each other.

One last thought to consider is that of creating a mission statement for your marriage. Churches create statements to reflect what their purpose or goal is. For two believers, a mission statement reflecting the spiritual purpose and direction for your marriage would tend to keep you on track spiritually as you move through the years in marriage. One book that can help you to do this is *Total Life Management* by Bob Shank (Multnomah Press, 1990).

Expectations and Goals

One other area for consideration is the entire realm of values and goals. One of the learning experiences in premarital counseling is having each person identify their expectations and goals for the marriage. By doing this in advance, it both clarifies what is important to each person and where they see the marriage heading.

You may want to do this yourself. Begin by each of you writing down 20 to 25 expectations you have for your potential partner as well as the marriage itself. Then look at each list and answer the following questions (they are written for an engaged couple):

1. Do we both have expectations in this area?

2. Do I have the same expectations for myself as I do for my fiancé? Why not?

3. How are our expectations of each other alike or different?

4. Whose expectations are stronger?

5. Whose expectations are most often met? Why? Because that person is older, stronger, more intelligent, male, more powerful?

6. Where do my expectations originate? From parents, books, church, siblings, the neighborhood where I grew up?

7. Are my expectations more worthy of fulfillment than my fiancé's?

8. Do all the people I know have the same expectations in a given area?

9. Do I have a "right" to my expectations?

10. Am I obligated to live up to my future spouse's expectations?[89]

Now take each expectation and answer the following:

1. Is this expectation I have of my fiancé supported by objective reality? Is it objectively true that he or she should act this way?

2. Am I hurt in any way, shape, or form if this expectation is not fulfilled?

3. Is this expectation essential to the attainment of any specific goal I have for my marriage?

4. What does this expectation do to my future spouse's perception of me?

5. Does this expectation help me achieve the kind of emotional responses I want for my spouse and me in marriage?[90]

Evaluating expectations is one way to work out those differences which could drive you apart. Yes, you can work out a solution which will satisfy both of you. You need to evaluate and clarify everything—and I mean *everything*! This includes food tastes, cooking styles, neatness level, time you retire at night and whether it's together or separately, taste in interior decoration, amount you spend on gifts, how important it is to you to remember birthdays and anniversaries, noise level in the home, frequency and type of TV programs, etc. These may sound mundane, but you wouldn't believe the number of marriages that fall apart because of these conflicts. If some item or issue isn't important or significant to you, but it is to your partner, then it needs to become more important to you. This is part of your growing and learning process.

Then look at your goals by writing them down and discussing them. Keep in mind that a goal is something you would like to achieve or see happen. It is a statement involving faith, for it tells of something we hope will happen in the future. "Faith is the substance of things hoped for" (Hebrews 11:1 KJV). We all have goals and dreams.

Goals give you a sense of direction. They are not what *will* be, but what you hope to attain. Because they are future-oriented, they can lift you from some of the difficulties of your present situation. Your focus can be upon positive hopes to come. As Christians we live in the present and future. Scripture admonishes us to have purposes and direction for our lives: "Forgetting the past and looking forward to what lies ahead, I strain to reach the end of the race" (Philippians 3:13,14 TLB); "A man's mind plans his way, but the Lord directs his steps" (Proverbs 16:9 RSV). Once we set goals, our steps can be directed by the Lord.

Goals will help you use your time more effectively, for they help you sort out what is important and what is not. If you know what you intend or need to do, it is much easier to keep from being sidetracked.

I have a list of demands placed upon my time for ministry to others. Some time ago I determined how much time I have available for my speaking ministry each month, what I feel needs to be accomplished during these times of ministry, and how best to accomplish the objectives. It is far easier now to evaluate requests and to say no to those that could detract me from the original God-directed goal.

As we decide upon goals, we need to realize that a goal is an event in the future that is accomplishable and measurable. If I say that I want to be a good swimmer, I am stating a purpose. If I say that I want to be able to swim six laps in an Olympic-size pool by July 1, I am stating a goal.

Here are the characteristics of well-stated goals:

1. *A goal should be stated in terms of the end result.* Example: Spend two hours a week in direct, face-to-face communication with my wife.

2. *A goal should be achievable in a definite time period.* Example: Spend two hours a week in direct, face-to-face communication with my wife by the end of February.

3. *A goal should be stated precisely in terms of quantities where applicable.* Example: Spend *two hours a week* in direct face-to-face communication with my wife by February.

4. *A goal should have one important goal or statement* rather than several.

How Do I Determine God's Will?

Having looked at these concerns, there is one other which is the deciding factor whether you feel you're compatible or not. The main question concerns God's will for your life and for your potential spouse. After all is said and done, just where does the will of God enter into all of this discussion? It's central, it's primary, and it's the most important aspect.

Let's consider some of the steps involved in this process. The first step is desiring the will of God for your life. In doing this it means surrendering your life to God and asking Him to be the directing agent. Derek Prince in his book *God Is a Match Maker* suggests the following concerning what happens when you surrender to God:

> In response to your surrender, God will do for you what you cannot achieve by any effort of your own will: He will renew your mind. He will change the way you think. This includes your goals, your values, your attitudes, and your priorities. All will be brought into line with those of God Himself.
>
> This inner change will find expression in your outward behavior. You will no longer be "conformed," acting like the unregenerate people all around you. Instead, you will be "transformed," and begin to demonstrate in your conduct the very nature and character of God.

Until you begin to experience this renewal of your mind, there are many wonderful things God has planned for you that you cannot discover. In Romans 8:7 Paul calls the old, unrenewed mind "the carnal mind," which is "enmity against God: for it is not subject to the law of God, neither indeed can it be" (KJV). God will not reveal His secrets or open up His treasures to a mind at enmity with Him. But when your mind is renewed, you will begin to discover all that God has planned for your life.

This unfolding of God's plan to your renewed mind will be progressive. Paul uses three words for it: good, pleasing, perfect.

Your first discovery will be that God's plan for you is always *good*. God never plans anything bad or harmful for any of His children. Not merely is God's plan *good*; it is also *pleasing*. Full surrender to God is the gateway into a life filled with challenges and pleasures that cannot be experienced in any other way. Over the years I have met many Christians who made this kind of surrender. I have never yet met one who regretted it. I know other Christians, on the other hand, who were challenged to make this surrender and refused. Almost without exception, they ended up frustrated and unfulfilled.

As you continue to progress in your discovery of God's plan, you will go beyond the *good* and the *pleasing* to the *perfect*. Fully embraced, God's plan is perfect. Complete. There are no omissions. It covers every area of your life, meets every need, satisfies every longing.

If marriage is part of God's plan for you, then you can trust Him to work out every detail, both for you and for the mate He has destined for you. He will bring you together with a person who is exactly suited to you that, together, you may experience marriage as God originally designed it. This will be on a level higher than the world has ever dreamed of.[91]

A second step is practicing obedience to God's will in every area of life. "Your word is a lamp to my feet and a light for my path" (Psalm 119:105 NIV).

The next step is developing relationships with believers, because marriages tend to develop out of existing relationships. This is a safeguard against marrying a non-Christian. "But if we walk in the light, as he is in the light, we have fellowship with one another . . ." (1 John 1:7 NIV).

A fourth guideline is to look for the Holy Spirit to lead you. Acknowledge your dependence on the Holy Spirit and be sensitive to His leading. Usually the Holy Spirit's prompting is quiet and gentle. "Those who are led by the Spirit of God are the sons of God" (Romans 8:14 NIV).

Another step is to watch what you allow into your heart as well as what you let out of your heart. If you indulge in fantasies or explicit sexual material, these can warp your perspective of what you are looking for. And developing relationships based on flirtations and shallow or physical involvements can keep you from finding the person you're seeking. "Above all else, guard your heart, for it is the wellspring of life" (Proverbs 4:23 NIV).

One of the most difficult steps is being willing to wait for God. We become impatient and take matters into our own hands. When you wait not only is your faith tested, but your motives undergo purification as well. It also builds the character quality of maturity. "The testing of your faith develops perseverance. Perseverance must finish its work so that you may be mature and complete . . . " (James 1:3,4 NIV). Waiting overcomes the erratic distortions which can be a part of moods and emotions. This verse is our reminder: "Since ancient times no one has heard, no ear has perceived, no eye has seen any God besides you, who acts on behalf of those who wait for him" (Isaiah 64:4 NIV).

Seek out the wisdom of other individuals, such as friends and family. Even secular research has shown the wisdom and value of doing this. "The way of a fool seems right to him, but a wise man listens to advice" (Proverbs 12:15 NIV). "A fool spurns his father's discipline, but whoever heeds correction shows prudence" (Proverbs 15:5 NIV).

Finally, remember that it is the Lord who gives the gift of a wife or husband. Approach every situation and decision with the question, "What is going to please the Lord?"[92] The psalmist described this in Psalm 37:4: "Delight yourself in the LORD; and he will give you the desires of your heart." "He who finds a wife finds what is good and receives favor from the LORD" (Proverbs 18:22 NIV).

You may be asking, "But are there any other guidelines or principles that I could follow to find God's will?" Here is another way of looking at this process.

Jim Dobson has suggested some basic principles for recognizing God's will for any area of one's life. These principles should be applied to any impressions that a person might have regarding marriage.

Is the impression scriptural? Guidance from God is always in accordance with His Word. If a Christian is considering marrying a non-Christian, there is no use in praying for God's will; the Scripture is clear concerning this situation. In searching the Scriptures, verses should be taken within context, not in a random sampling.

Is it providential? Every impression ought to be considered in the light of providential circumstances. Are necessary doors opening or closing? Is God speaking through events?

Is the impression reasonable? Does the impression make sense? Is it consistent with the character of God to require it?

If a person has numerous mixed feelings about marrying the other individual, if there is no peace over the upcoming event, and if the majority of friends and relatives are opposed to the wedding, the decision ought to be reconsidered.[93]

In yet a little different way of looking at this, one counselor identifies five voices which the believer can listen to for affirmation of his decision-making ability. He shared these principles in one of his messages to his congregation. No one single voice should carry the total weight of choosing a life partner. The first voice is that of Scripture itself. The balance that Scripture brings to our attempts at choosing a life partner leads us to balance all areas of our life. It is easy to be infatuated with many individuals with whom we come in contact. It is also easy to think that we have fallen head over heels in love with those same individuals. We can be attracted to believers and nonbelievers alike. Scripture itself helps us to get a perspective on the kind of person the believer is to marry. It clearly states: "Do not be bound together with unbelievers; for what partnership have righteousness and lawlessness, or what fellowship has light with darkness?" (2 Corinthians 6:14 NASB). The believer consequently has no real freedom, except to choose a believer as his partner.

The second voice is that "still small voice" which is God's Spirit guiding us from within, that inner feeling that says, "What you are about to do is OK." It is important to remember that in determining God's will for so important a decision as the choice of a life partner, each voice is carefully checked with the others.

The third voice is based upon providential and experiential circumstances. This voice is heard as we move through courtship and see more and more that this person may truly be the partner God has called to be our companion through life, the parent of our child, and the one who will provide for and nurture us for a lifetime.

The fourth voice is often locked in a cell constructed from our own emotions. It has been said that when love comes in, reason flies out the door. We do need to give deep and prayerful consideration to the individual whom we may choose, and it is our choice ultimately as to who will be our life partner.

The fifth voice may actually be a chorus of voices. It is the affirmation provided by other individuals who play significant roles in our lives.

Think about all of these suggestions. Remember to integrate them with how you are going to build compatibility with that special person.

Remember that God wants to fulfill every plan and purpose He has for your life. Consider also a few more words from Derek Prince: "Remember from now on you do not make your own decisions. You find out God's decisions and make them yours."

There is one more thing to remember, too: "God gives His best to those who leave the choice to Him."[94]

The Second Time Around

"Norm, I'm getting married... again. What do I need to know?" This is a common question, an imposing question, and an overwhelming question. It certainly needs and deserves an answer. You may be the one marrying again or you may be marrying someone who is getting married again. Or it could be this chapter doesn't pertain to you at all. If not, it may be useful to one of your friends.

What is shared in the next several pages is not meant to discourage or dishearten you about a marriage in which one person has been married before. It's simply to prepare you beforehand so you can be fully aware and in charge of your life and your new relationship.

If you're ready to marry again it means you have emerged from that dark, cluttered, frightening valley which most people experience during and after a divorce. Hopefully you've been able to rearrange your life without assaults from your former spouse. So many divorces

I've seen remind me of a country that divides into two, but one carries on guerrilla warfare attacks upon the other.

In many cases, divorce can leave you with a terrible sense of failure and guilt. Finding your way back to stability can leave you either shattered, questioning your sanity and your abilities, or it can leave you stronger and wiser. You won't be the same person you were in your first marriage. The time between marriages is an extremely significant time in your life, especially for your future. Recuperation from any serious trauma is never easy, and for a while it often involves two steps forward and one step back.[95]

Stages of Recuperation

Following your divorce you very possibly went through four different stages. The first one was "Remembering the Pain." At that point in time, if a thought about a new relationship came to mind it could have been like pouring salt in an open cut—it hurt too much. Your divorce may have been too recent and painful. Whenever you saw a couple together who appeared happy, an entire onslaught of feelings emerged. You felt like half a person.

Then you moved into a new stage of "Single Again Acceptance." Your pain diminished, and you held your head above water to see what this new world was like. You discovered you were not alone, but you may have felt fragile. Question after question came to mind— "How do I relate to others again? Where did I go wrong? Can I attract someone? Who would want me?" A new and deep commitment was inconceivable. The greatest danger at that time was sex. To feel wanted and close again could have conflicted with your Christian values.

In the third stage of "Searching and Selective," you began to feel whole again and you became interested in finding someone. You were comfortable with time alone, and you made yourself more available. But you would tend to evaluate each new person carefully. You were not ready for a commitment yet, but you may have wanted to move toward a close relationship.

The last stage is where you said, "Yes, I'm ready!" You began functioning as a whole person, and marriage began to look more attractive than remaining single. You allowed a relationship to proceed at its own pace. You were ready for a commitment when the risk of that step was less to be feared than not taking it. Often it takes three to four years after a divorce for this to occur. If it happens in the first year, it's too soon. Waiting gives you the opportunity to learn to find and love a whole person rather than half a person.[96]

I think it would be safe to say that every person entering a second marriage after a divorce is hoping and expecting it to be better than the first one. Hopefully this desire will prompt them to take every step possible to make that wish a reality. But think about Jim Smoke's comments on new spouses:

> Here are a few hidden expectations of new spouses that have been shared with me over the years. If any of them sound like yours, get them out of hiding:
>
> 1. My new spouse will make me far happier than my former spouse did.
>
> 2. My new spouse will be totally different from my former spouse.
>
> 3. My new spouse will always understand me.
>
> 4. My new spouse will have none of the bad habits of my former spouse.
>
> 5. My new spouse will be a better parent than my former spouse.

6. My new spouse will never disappoint me.

7. My new spouse will never handle money as poorly as my former spouse.

8. My new spouse will make me a better person and make me happy.

9. My new spouse will make all the pain and hurt from my previous marriage go away.

10. My new spouse is perfect.

If any about-to-be current second-marriage spouses knew that the above were expectations for them, they would probably leave the country.[97]

Hope for the Second Marriage

I've been encouraged by those who have spent months preparing by attending second marriage premarital preparation courses as well as being involved in individual premarital counseling sessions. But other individuals just seem to waltz into their next marriage assuming it will be better. But a second marriage is not any easier than a first; it is harder. Not only that, it's much more complicated. If you thought your first marriage took effort, you may be surprised what happens now.

In a first marriage, you didn't have to share your partner with anyone else, nor did your partner have to share you with anyone. But if either or both have children, you may end up with 50 to 75 percent less time and energy to devote to the building of your new marriage. And in one sense a second marriage is similar to a first marriage—the initial year is the most important when it comes to bonding and building a relationship. But with less time available, it may take much longer.

As you approach a second marriage, have you given any consideration as to why the divorce rate for second marriages is higher than for first marriages? There are some identifiable reasons. It may help to keep these in mind. Here are some of the factors that cause second marriages to fail.

Frequently a person's second marriage is meant to punish the first partner and absolve the punishing partner of blame.

There is pressure to make the second marriage work. There may be feelings of having to make up for the lacking areas in the first marriage, and a number of "musts" and "shoulds" are set up which can cripple the marriage.

Rushing into a new marriage is one of the best ways for it to fail. Some second marriages fail because of a repetition compulsion—choosing the same kind of partner again or repeating some of the same bad habits.

Failure to learn from the first time around will contaminate a new marriage.[98]

Characteristics of a Second Marriage

A second marriage is different from a first for a number of reasons. In a remarriage there is usually another cast of characters in addition to the two of you, and the possibilities for problems are unlimited. You are also becoming involved with your spouse's family of origin, their previous spouse and their family, children from the first marriage, and also friends. The relationships expand as you each bring your own children into the arena. You're related now emotionally and by law. What if the previous ex of your new spouse remarries? You'll hear about them as well as have them in your life, too. In a sense you could be marrying into one huge extended family with a number of people neither of you cares about. But you're stuck with them!

And there are numerous outside pressures that will be new to you. They'll come at you from all sides from parents, neighbors, families, jobs, school, and former family members. You'll hear comments which range from positive to negative. "Oh, you're Bob's new wife. Well, I hope you can handle his kids better than 'she' did," or "Well, Jim, I certainly hope you give Laura a hand with the finances. I think that would help her get her accounts in order as well." Even your new spouse's parents may have some advice or warning statements for you. There will be others who resent you, dislike you, compare you, love you, ignore you, and accept you. The possibilities are endless. Some could praise you, frighten you, undermine you, or welcome you with open arms. I've seen it all. One remarried man said, "My former wife is still in my life and tries to mess it up. She poisons the children's minds about my new wife and has spread stories about her to the neighbors. Now the kids wonder who they are to believe!"

Keep in mind that in a first marriage there are fewer people involved than in a remarriage, and the feelings are much less complicated.

When you first married, how did your parents respond? Probably they were either sad or glad. With a second marriage there may be hesitation, reservations, or worry over whether this marriage will work out or not. And if there are going to be stepchildren involved, the apprehension can be even greater on their part. Consider this possibility: Your children or stepchildren-to-be will wonder where they fit into this family and how they will get along with the new family members. I've seen second marriages dissolve because one of the children hated the stepparent so much he would never let the parents be alone while he was in the house. He would interrupt their conversations and actually step between them when they were talking.

Perhaps your parents or your ex-partner's parents will be upset about your plans to remarry and worry over not seeing the grandchildren as much. Perhaps the ex-spouse will be concerned that you'll want custody, financial help, and visitation changes. Or perhaps they will want these things! Perhaps an ex-spouse will give you a wedding present of having your children or your new partner's children come to live with you. It's happened before.

Keep in mind that people bring routines into a remarriage that were developed with a former spouse. A new spouse may be expected to know and accept these routines. What if you or your new spouse has a close relationship with a parent of a former spouse and wants to maintain that relationship? How will that affect a new marriage? People tend to bring memories into a remarriage, both positive and negative. When everything is going well with your new partner, your memories of the previous relationship are negative. You recall the shortcomings. But when things are not going well with your new partner, you may tend to idealize the former relationship. Remarriages can be fertile ground for comparison. And if either or both of you bring children into the relationship, there will be a multitude of adjustments.

Let me make some initial suggestions based on 30 years of counseling married, divorced, and premarital individuals and couples. I make these suggestions out of a desire for you to have the fulfilling relationship you are seeking. It could very well be that the next series of suggestions, comments, and questions could be bothersome or even offensive, but they are meant to bring a sense of realism into your future.

If your former spouse has not remarried, have you considered or attempted reconciliation, or is that door thoroughly closed?

Is getting married again something that you believe is the will of God for your life? Could you explain the reasons for your answer?

Have you participated in an intensive divorce recovery workshop program and completed all the requested assignments? Before beginning any new relationship, this is a must. It will take time and effort on your part to complete this, but it's essential for recovery. The difficulty is often finding such an opportunity. Many smaller churches or even middle-sized ones don't have such a ministry, and in small communities it's even more difficult to find this kind of workshop. Fortunately a complete divorce recovery program is now available on video with an accompanying workbook called *Divorce Care*. (Details on where to obtain these materials can be obtained from Christian Marriage Enrichment at 1-800-875-7560.) Even if you have never been married before, if you are marrying someone who has, it would be beneficial for you to sit in on a recovery program or use the *Divorce Care* series. The greater your depth of understanding about the complexity of divorce and recovery, the greater your chances of developing a healthy relationship.

By the way, if you have experienced a divorce and have recovered, be cautious about dating someone who is recently divorced. They tend to look to you to rescue them, and you may be dealing with a rebounder.

How Do You Know If You're Ready?

A big question to answer is, Are you ready for remarriage? Many people who divorce live with fear and have difficulty trusting. Chances are your trust with your former partner was broken, and you may struggle to trust anyone again. And you may struggle with the fear of having the next relationship be a repeat of the first. Trust is built slowly. You need to learn to trust your own decisions, judgments, and feelings. As you do, fear will be crowded out.[99]

Do others feel you're ready for remarriage? If you haven't asked your closest friends and family members, do so. Ask them for specific reasons as well. Are you realistic when it comes to making a new marriage work if there are children involved? Keep in mind it takes at least five to six years for a blended family to blend.

Some of the couples I work with who are considering remarriage wonder if they are really free from the influences of their previous marriage enough to remarry. If you answer the following questions in the affirmative, perhaps you need to reconsider getting married again at this time:

> Does this new potential spouse resemble your former spouse in their appearance?
>
> Does the personality quality that you value so much in this new person seem to be the one your former spouse lacked?
>
> Do the same conflict(s) that were in your previous marriage also exist in this relationship?
>
> Do you hold resentment against yourself or your former spouse for what happened in your marriage?
>
> Did this relationship begin as an affair while you were previously married?
>
> Do you resist or rebel against anything that reminds you of your previous spouse or your way of life together?
>
> Do you spend a lot of time thinking about what is going on in the life of your previous spouse?
>
> Are you searching for someone who is a clone of your former partner but without defects?
>
> Sometimes postponing the decision to marry again is helpful for recovery and change to occur.[100]

Have you taken time to find out everything you can about your new love's former marriage? What did they like and dislike about their former spouse, and what are their expectations of you because of that? Don't be afraid to ask, "What did you do wrong?" By the same token, be willing to share what you did wrong if you were married before. Listen to your partner when they talk about their first marriage. They're not just sharing history, but information that will influence your marriage. Fears and hurts which took years to accumulate won't disappear overnight. Bringing issues out into the open is healthy. Be sure you look at your own issues if you were married before.

Why Am I Getting Remarried?

Perhaps you're already in a new relationship and are hoping that it will lead to marriage. Jim Smoke in his helpful book *Growing In Remarriage* raises some cautionary guidelines concerning various types of Rescue Motivations for marriage. This happens quite frequently in second marriages. We discussed several of these in chapter 9, including emotional rescue, relational rescue, and financial rescue. Some of the same reasons that keep us in a relationship too long can push us into a relationship too soon.

In addition to the other forms of rescue, you will face the sex issue again. Sexual rescue is a problem most single-again persons will have to face. The concern is twofold: "Will I ever have sex again now that I am single?" and "Will I and can I be celibate until I marry again?" This becomes the big pursuit for many people, and some have found this pressure prompting their move toward marriage. But the sex drive by itself is not sufficient reason for getting married. Celibacy and a biblical pattern of living is possible and is more commonly practiced than you might believe.

One other form of rescue is worth noting—parental rescue. A custodial parent of one, two, three, or four children can be worn to a frazzle. Many second marriages have come about because the parent wanted another parent more than they wanted a spouse. Keep in mind that a biological parent will always have stronger ties and more of an emotional investment in their children than a stepparent. A second marriage will never rescue you from being the primary parent.[101]

Fortunately, we are able to take advantage of the wealth of information that has been accumulated over the years about the adjustment issues in remarriage. It's much simpler when there are no children coming into the new marriage. But many remarriages have multiple children on both sides.

If you or your new spouse are bringing children into a new marriage, hopefully there is a healthy, cooperative relationship between the biological parent and their ex. But if it is more of an adversarial relationship, you or your new spouse may need to formulate some form of foreign policy of conduct toward the former spouse. The purpose of such a policy is as follows:

—to prevent a former spouse from draining emotional or material resources from your new marriage.

—to prevent your former marriage from interfering and having a negative influence on your new marriage.

—to keep your former spouse's responses from hurting the children in your new marriage.

—to attempt to build some type of healthy, mature interaction between the former spouses.

You or your new spouse may need to be firm in your responses, unavailable at times when the former spouse tries to make contact. Make it very clear that the new relationship comes first and be willing to help your new partner cope with the former one.[102]

Major Adjustment Issues

Here are some of the major issues of remarriage families. These are not presented to threaten or scare you but to enlighten you and help you make the necessary preparations and adjustments needed to have a successful relationship. You may even be surprised by some of these items, but they have been found to be very significant.

One of the issues is what name is used for the new parent. Each family has to work out a comfort level for each member.

First of all, *what does a child call you*—an "additional" or "substitute" parent? Children often prefer to think in terms of "new father" and "old father" or "real father." Or they could say "first" or "second." Stepchildren not only have difficulty with the name "step-" but they may also struggle with their mother's new name which is now different from their own.

The *expression of love and affection to a new parent* is not easy to resolve, because it involves feelings of loyalty or alliance to their own absent parent. A stepparent will probably experience both positive and negative feelings from the children. Some children may become close to the stepparent and others remain distant.

The *loss of the natural parent* will generate a grief reaction. If family members are still working through their grief response when a new (or several) family members enter the family, both the recovery and the bonding in the new relationship will be delayed. Most people in our society do not know how to grieve, nor do those around them know how to assist them in the process.

Many remarriage family members believe that *feelings of love and affection* can develop easily in the family relationships. This does not usually happen, and a high level of expectation for this occurring can generate a strong sense of disillusionment in the new marriage. It will take a significant amount of time. If you are going to become a blended family, consider these things that will probably be part of your experience.

What usually happens when families are blended is:

1. You will spend a great deal of time patching the wounds of fragmented family members.

2. You will come to dread that part of the holidays when children pass each other in airports.

3. You will have more spare toys, blankets, towels, and sleeping bags in your home than you know what to do with.

4. Some days, you will wonder what children belong to what parent on what planet.

5. You will quickly tire of being the "bad guy" stepparent.

6. You will want all children to become wards of the court when it comes to dispensing discipline.

7. You will tire of hearing children say, "My real father [mother] said I could do . . ."

8. You will be loved and unloved in the same minute some days.

9. You will expect God to give all stepparents a castle free of kids in heaven.[103]

A fifth issue is the *disappointment that children experience* when their dreams and fantasies of their parents reconciling fail to materialize. The fact of a second marriage puts an end to any of their hopes. Even years after a divorce, children entertain these dreams. If children are especially close to the noncustodial parent and hang onto dreams of their parents working it out, the new marriage is likely to experience difficulties.

The number-one problem in remarriages in which there are children are the *conflicts over discipline*. Some stepparents stay inattentive and disengaged—that doesn't work. Some become actively involved and overly restrictive—that doesn't work. Others remain tentative, and that doesn't work. What does work, then? The approach that works is a slow, gentle, flexible approach in which a friendship is developed to gain a child's participation. The biological parent, however, should take the lead with the stepparent supporting them. But this only works when you talk about it in advance.

Another adjustment is *sibling conflicts*. If the children are still upset and angry over their parents' divorce, there will be friction between the step-siblings. These relationships are critical to the success of blended families. The better the relationships between step-siblings, the better the total family harmony.

Within a blended family you will find *competition* for a time. There is usually an unequal time distribution, and the children often feel they have been forced to choose between the stepparent and the biological parent.

The greater the number of newly acquired family members, the greater the *complexity of the relationships*. The more people there are, the harder it is to find yourself in the system. As one new husband and stepfather said, "It's like I married into a crowd that's always milling around, and it's not only hard to know where you fit, it's also hard to get some alone time."

A remarriage family also has a *greater potential for inappropriate sexual behavior*. This may occur between step-siblings or, unfortunately, between a stepparent and a stepchild. Sometimes the sexual tension, fantasies, and anxieties can create tension and anger which can disrupt normal day-to-day functioning.

Children experience *emotional turmoil* when they shift back and forth from their home to their other biological parent and back again. They will experience disruption for several days, because the exit and entry time expands beyond the time of visitation. There's both a time of preparation and a time of recovery after the return home. Often this disruption is observable in school. Feelings of guilt, loss, and a need to grieve are normal responses to this adjustment.

Because a remarriage with children means instant family, *any marital problems are going to be compounded*. There is no opportunity to consider the marital relationship first. But if the stepparent-children relationship works out, it has a positive effect upon the marriage.

Money problems could be an issue, and it's common to have conflicts over child support, spousal support, wills, trusts, distribution of future assets, payment for a daughter's wedding, prenuptials, etc.

One other concern is the *continued influence of the noncustodial parent in child-rearing practices*. If all the parents do not cooperate, a child feels this stress. The sooner the remarriage follows the divorce, the more competition there is between parents.[104]

In spite of all the adjustments, problems, and multiple relationships, a remarriage can be a fulfilling time in which each person can find what they were always seeking in marriage. By planning, praying, and being persistent in working through issues, it can work. I've seen it happen time and time again. Make it happen. It's your choice.

APPENDIX A

Interview Questions for New Relationships

What special memories do you have about your childhood?

How did you get along with each of your parents? What were they like?

What did you like and dislike about your parents?

What were your hurts and disappointments as a child?

What were your hobbies and favorite games?

How did you usually get into trouble?

How did you usually try to get out of trouble?

What did you enjoy about school and its activities?

What pets did you have? Which were your favorites and why?

What did you dream about doing when you were older?

Did you like yourself as a child? Why or why not?

Did you like yourself as a teenager? Why or why not?

What were your talents and special abilities?

What awards and special achievements did you win?

Did you have a nickname?

Who were your close friends? Where are they today?

What would you do on a hot summer afternoon?

Describe the area where you grew up—people, neighborhood, etc.

What were you afraid of? Do you have any of those fears today?

How did you get along with your brothers and/or sisters? If you had none, which relative were you closest to?

What was your first date?

Who did you date and for how long? Where did you go on dates?

How did you feel when you liked someone and that person didn't care for you?

What was your spiritual life like as a child? As an adolescent?

How has being an adult (19 on) changed your life?

How are you different today than you were ten years ago?

What have been your greatest disappointments? How have you handled them?

What have you learned from them that you would want me to learn?

What parts of your childhood would you like to relive?

What do you remember about your first day of school?

Did you enjoy school? Why or why not? What was your favorite grade and who were your favorite teachers?

At what age did you first like the opposite sex?

What was your birth order in your family?

Did you have enough money in your youth? Enough clothing?

Who were your other dates or steadies? What did you like and dislike about each one?

What jobs have you held?

What is the extent of your education and job experiences? What were your emotional reactions to jobs, fellow employees, and bosses? What were your ambitions?

What do you think your natural gifts are?

What do you consider your strong points? Weak points?

What is your medical history?

What is your favorite holiday, music, television program, and pastime?

What is your definition of an ideal spouse?

Do you like pets? Which ones?

Who are the five most important people in your life?

Which Christian leaders or writers have influenced you?

Who are your friends?

Where would you like to live? What country, state, city, house, apartment?

What are your views on aging?

Who were the Christians in your family?

What has been the best year of your life? Why?

Who educated you in sex? What were your sexual experiences? What is your standard for sexual expression at this time in your life?

What are your political views?

What do you enjoy reading? Watching on TV?

Have you ever had a child? Do you want children?

What is the first thing that you can remember?

Who were your favorite relatives?

APPENDIX B

Premarital Resources

There are a variety of approaches to premarital preparation. The most thorough and helpful is the individualized approach in which you meet as a couple with a minister, qualified lay couple, or counselor for six to eight hours. It is helpful to attend group classes as an additional source of support, but group sessions by themselves are not nearly as effective as the individual-couple approach. Ask detailed questions about the approach including testing and supplemental resources. You will be asked to take a battery of tests. My own recommendation for tests and resources are as follows:

For the Engaged Couple

Testing

Prepare, Taylor Johnson Temperament Analysis, Family History Analysis, and the Meyers-Briggs Type Indicator

Books

Before You Say I Do by Norm Wright, Harvest House Publishers (one per person)

So You're Getting Married by Norm Wright, Regal Books (one per person)

If Only He Knew by Gary Smalley, Zondervan (for the man)

For Better, For Best by Gary Smalley, Zondervan (for the woman)

How to Change Your Spouse Without Ruining Your Marriage chapters 4-9,13 by Oliver and Wright, Servant Publications (for both)

Getting Your Sex Life Off to a Great Start by Cliff and Joyce Penner, Word Publishers

Tapes

Before the Wedding Night by Ed Wheat (optional)

Your Finances in Changing Times by Larry Burkett

Tender Warrior by Stu Weber (for the man)

All of these resources can be obtained from:

Christian Marriage Enrichment
17821 17th St. #190
Tustin, CA 92680
1-800-875-7560

Notes

CHAPTER 1: Marriage—Is It the Answer for You?

1. Miriam Arond and Samuel L. Parker, M.D., *The First Year of Marriage* (New York: Warner Books, 1987), pp. 9-10, adapted.
2. Ibid., pp. 307, adapted.
3. Ibid., pp. 342-43, adapted.
4. Ibid., p. 343, adapted.
5. Claire Cloninger, *When the Glass Slipper Doesn't Fit and the Silver Spoon Is in Someone Else's Mouth* (Dallas: Word Publishers, 1993), p. 93. All rights reserved.
6. Mike Mason, *The Mystery of Marriage* (Portland, OR: Multnomah Press, 1985), p. 56.
7. Michael J. McManus, *Marriage Savers* (Grand Rapids, MI: Zondervan, 1993), p. 23, adapted.
8. Susan Page, *If I'm So Wonderful, Why Am I Still Single?* (New York: Bantam Books, 1988), pp. 19-20, adapted.
9. McManus, pp. 92-93, adapted.
10. Jim Talley and Bobbie Reed, *Too Close, Too Soon* (Nashville: Thomas Nelson Publishers, 1982), p. 21.
11. Ibid.
12. Bob Burns and Tom Whiteman, *The Fresh Start Divorce Recovery Workshop* (Nashville, TN: Thomas Nelson, 1992), p. 144.
13. Steve Wilke, Dave Jackson, and Neta Jackson, *When We Can't Talk Anymore* (Wheaton, IL: Tyndale, 1992), p. 11.
14. Donald Harvey, *The Drifting Marriage* (Old Tappan, NJ: Fleming H. Revell, 1988), p. 213.
15. Neil Clark Warren, *Finding the Love of Your Life* (Colorado Springs: Focus on the Family, 1992), p. 171. All rights reserved. International copyright secured. Used by permission of Focus on the Family.
16. Second Edition by Robert O. Blood, Jr., Copyright © 1969 by The Free Press, a Division of Simon & Schuster, pp. 10-11. Reprinted with permission of the publisher.
17. John Gottman, PhD., *Why Marriages Succeed or Fail* (New York: Simon & Schuster, 1994), pp. 32-57, adapted.
18. Harvey, p. 44.

CHAPTER 2: "I'm Afraid of a Relationship"

19. M. Blaine Smith, *Should I Get Married?* (Downers Grove, IL: Inter-varsity Press, 1990), pp. 190-97, adapted.
20. Tim Timmons and Charlie Hedges, *Call It Love or Call It Quits* (Fort Worth, TX: Worthy Publishing, 1988), pp. 122-28, adapted.
21. David Burns, *Feeling Good* (New York: Signet Books, 1980), p. 258.
22. H. Norman Wright, *Afraid No More* (Downers Grove, IL: Tyndale, 1989), p.76-77, adapted.
23. Ibid., pp. 54-56, adapted.

CHAPTER 3: If You Haven't Recovered—Wait!

24. Stephen Gullo, Ph.D., and Connie Church, *Love Shock: How to Recover from a Broken Heart and Live Again* (New York: Bantam Books, 1988), pp. 63-75, adapted.
25. Dr. Zev Wanderer and Tracy Cobot, Ph.D., *Letting Go* (Dell Books, 1978), pp. 11-12, adapted.
26. Gullo and Church, p. 26, adapted.
27. "Good-bye to Love" by John Bettis, music by Richard Carpenter. Copyright 1972 by ALMO Music Corp., Hammer and Nails Music.
28. Anita Brock, *Divorce Recovery* (Fort Worth, TX: Worthy Publishing, 1988), p. 20, adapted.
29. Ibid., pp. 19-23, adapted.
30. Dr. Susan Forward, *Obsessive Love* (New York: Bantam Books, 1991), pp. 48, 76, adapted.
31. Dr. Zev Wanderer and Tracy Cabot, *Letting Go* (New York: Ell Publishing, 1978), pp. 27-28, adapted.
32. Wanderer and Cabot, *Letting Go*, pp. 97-100, adapted.
33. Brock, *Divorce Recovery*, pp. 39-45, adapted.
34. Gullo and Church, pp. 99-109, adapted.

CHAPTER 4: "Why Am I Not Married Now, and What Can I Do About It?"

35. Tim Stafford, *A Love Story* (Grand Rapids, MI: Zondervan, 1977), pp. 91-93.
36. Charles Cerling, "Is Marriage For You?: A High School Curriculum," *Marriage and Family Resource Newsletter*, vol. 3, no. 6 (June/July 1977).
37. Dr. Larry E. Davis, *Black and Single* (Chicago: Noble Press, 1993), p. 79-80, adapted.
38. Margaret Kent, *How to Marry the Man of Your Choice* (New York: Warner Books, 1984), p. 66, adapted.
39. Davis, pp. 24-27.

40. Robert F. Stahmann and William J. Hiebert, *Premarital Counseling* (Lexington, MA: Lexington Books, 1980), p. 20-21.
41. J. Richard Udry, *The Social Context of Marriage*, 3rd ed. (New York: Lippincott, 1974), p. 157, adapted.

CHAPTER 5: "Where Do I Meet Them and What Do I Say?"

42. Susan Page, *If I'm So Wonderful, Why Am I Still Single?* (New York: Bantam Books, 1988), pp. 41-42, adapted.
43. Judith Sills, Ph.D., *How to Stop Looking For Someone Perfect and Find Someone to Love* (New York: Ballantine Books, 1984), pp. 35-38, adapted.
44. *Equally Yoked* (Los Angeles office)
    12069 Ventura Place, Suite B
    Studio City, CA 91604
    (818) 506-5122
45. Christian Singles Connection
    P.O. Box 4927
    Anaheim, CA 92803
    1-800-560-5494 or 1-800-556-1888
46. Christian Singles Confidential Introductions
    16168 Beach Blvd. #140
    Huntington Beach, CA 92647
    (714) 375-0400

CHAPTER 6: Relationships: Short-term, Long-term, and None

47. Michael S. Broder, Ph.D., *The Art of Staying Together* (New York: Hyperion, 1993), pp. 125-26, adapted.
48. Ibid., p. 128, adapted.
49. Darryl E. Owens, from *The Orlando Sentinel*. "Bachelor Fad," *Missoulian*, June 20, 1994, section B, Families, p. 1, adapted.
50. Broder, pp. 127-31, adapted.
51. Dr. Susan Forward, *Obsessive Love* (New York: Bantam Books, 1991), pp. 23-24, adapted.
52. Forward, p. 7, adapted.
53. Forward, pp. 11-12, adapted.
54. Broder, p. 30, adapted.
55. David G. Myers, Ph.D., *The Pursuit of Happiness* (New York: William Morrow & Co., 1992), pp. 168-69, adapted.

CHAPTER 7: "How Do I Know If I'm in Love?"

56. M. Scott Peck, *The Road Less Traveled* (New York: Simon & Schuster, Inc., 1978), p. 91. Reprinted by permission of Simon & Schuster, Inc.

57. *Webster's New World Dictionary, Third College Edition* (New York. Prentice Hall), p. 691.
58. Susan Page, *If I'm So Wonderful, Why Am I Still Single?* p. 106, adapted.
59. *Webster's New Collegiate Dictionary* (New York: Prentice Hall), p. 916.
60. Quoted in *Love Gone Wrong* by Thomas Whiteman and Randy Peterson (Nashville: Thomas Nelson Publishers, 1994), p. 41.
61. M. Scott Peck, *The Road Less Traveled* (New York: Simon & Schuster, 1978), p. 84. Reprinted by permission of Simon & Schuster, Inc.
62. Dr. Phillip Captain, professor at Liberty University, Lynchburg, VA. Workshop presentation at the International Congress on Christian Counseling in Atlanta, GA, 1992.
63. Thomas F. Jones, *Sex and Love When You're Single Again* (Nashville: Thomas Nelson Publishers, 1990), pp. 93-96, adapted.
64. Neil Clark Warren, Ph.D., *Finding the Love of Your Life* (Colorado Springs: Focus on the Family, 1992), pp. 81-82. All rights reserved. International copyright secured. Used by permission of Focus on the Family.
65. Ibid., p. 84.
66. Bernard I. Murstein, *Paths to Marriage* (San Mateo, CA: Sage Publications, 1986), p. 110.
67. Warren, pp. 97-99, adapted.
68. Paul Tournier. Original source unknown.
69. David L. Leuche, *The Relationship Manual,* (Columbia, MD: The Relationship Institute, 1981), p. 3, adapted.
70. Walter Trobisch, *I Married You* (New York: Harper & Row Publishers, Inc., 1975), pp. 75-77.
71. William J. McRae, *Preparing for Your Marriage* (Grand Rapids, MI: Zondervan Publishing House, 1980), p. 37. Used by permission of Zondervan Publishing House.
72. Jones, pp. 86-87, adapted.
73. Leo F. Buscaglia, *Loving Each Other* (New York: Random House, Inc.—Fawcett Columbine, 1984), pp. 46-50. Used by permission

CHAPTER 8: Counterfeit Love Styles

74. Charles Swindoll, *The Quest for Character* (Portland, OR: Multnomah Press, 1988), adapted from p. 67.
75. Charles Swindoll, *Improving Your Serve* (Waco, TX: Word Books, 1981), pp. 116-17. All rights reserved.
76. Karen Kayser, *When Love Dies* (New York: The Guilford Press 1993), pp. 93-94, adapted.

77. Dr. Les Parrott III, *Love's Unseen Enemy* (Grand Rapids, MI: Zondervan Publishing House, 1994), pp. 121-30, 184-85, adapted. Used by permission of Zondervan Publishing House.
78. Ibid., pp. 143-48, 185, adapted.
79. Ibid., p. 158.
80. Ibid., pp. 158-59, 186, adapted.

CHAPTER 9: When You're Dating the Wrong Person

81. Margaret Kent, *How to Marry the Man of Your Choice* (New York: Warner Books, 1984), p. 66, adapted.
82. Jim Smoke, *Growing in Remarriage* (Old Tappan, NY: Fleming H. Revell, 1990), p. 47.
83. Ibid., pp. 47-51, adapted.

CHAPTER 10: "Are We Compatible?"

84. *Webster's New World Dictionary, Third College Edition*, Victoria Neufeldt, ed. (New York: Prentice Hall, 1994), p. 284.
85. Jeanette C. Laver and Robert H. Laver, *Till Death Do Us Part* (New York: Harrington Park Press, 1986), pp. 153-54, adapted.
86. Blaine Smith, *Should I Get Married?* (Downers Grove, IL: Intervarsity Press, 1990), p. 92.
87. Gary J. Oliver and H. Norman Wright, *How to Change Your Spouse* (Ann Arbor, MI: Servant Publications, 1994), pp. 116-21, 174-83. Used with permission.
88. Max Lucado, *Six Hours One Friday* (Portland, OR: Multnomah Press, 1989), p. 36.
89. H. Norman Wright, *So You're Getting Married* (Ventura, CA: Regal Books, 1985), p. 108. Used by permission.
90. Ibid., p. 109.
91. Derek Prince with Ruth Prince, *God Is a Match Maker* (Grand Rapids, MI: Chosen Books, 1986), pp. 54-56.
92. Ibid., pp. 70-80, adapted.
93. James Dobson, *Dr. Dobson Talks About God's Will* (Glendale, CA: Regal Books, 1974), pp. 13-21, adapted.
94. Prince, p. 57.

CHAPTER 11: The Second Time Around

95. Leslie Altridge Westoff, *The Second Time Around* (New York: The Viking Press, 1977), pp. 24-27, adapted.
96. Mel Krantzler, *Learning to Love Again* (New York: Thomas Y. Crowell Co., 1977), pp. 102-14, adapted.
97. Jim Smoke, *Growing in Remarriage* (Old Tappan, NJ: Revell, 1990), p. 88.

98. Jean Baer, *The Second Wife* (New York: Doubleday Co., 1972), pp. 209-13, adapted.
99. Jim Smoke, pp. 35-40, adapted.
100. Frederick F. Flach, *A New Marriage* (New York: McGraw-Hill Book Co., 1978), pp. 65-66, adapted.
101. Smoke, pp. 47-54, adapted.
102. Flach, pp. 137-42, adapted.
103. Smoke, p. 92.
104. "Twenty Major Issues in Remarriage Families" (*Journal of Counseling and Development*, July/August 1992, vol. 70), pp. 709-17, adapted.